STUDY GUIDE

Kenrick S. Thompson
Arkansas State University Mountain Home

MARRIAGES AND FAMILIES

FOURTH EDITION

Nijole Benokraitis

Prentice Hall, Upper Saddle River, New Jersey 07458

©2002 by PEARSON EDUCATION, INC.
Upper Saddle River, New Jersey 07458

ISBN 0-13-060892-0

Printed in the United States of America

CONTENTS

PREFACE

This study guide is designed to accompany **Marriages And Families: Changes, Choices, and Constraints, 4e, by Nijole V. Benokraitis.**

Each chapter in this manual includes chapter objectives, a chapter overview, current applications designed to stimulate your thinking about relevant concepts and issues, fill-in-the-blank questions targeted at the key terms in the chapter, and sample multiple choice questions. An answer key for the fill-in and multiple choice items concludes each chapter.

I hope that the contents of this study guide will help you to better understand your readings in the Benokraitis text, to improve your performance on examinations, and derive more enjoyment from the marriage and family course.

Kenrick S. Thompson, Ph.D.
kthompson@brook.asumh.edu

THE CHANGING FAMILY

CHAPTER OBJECTIVES

Based upon their reading and careful consideration of Chapter One, students should:

1. be familiar with the various definitions of the family and how these definitions mirror the changing functions of the American family.

2. be able to identify the basic functions of the family: legitimizing sexual activity, bearing and raising children, providing emotional support to family members, and establishing members' place in society.

3. understand the "rules" of marriage and family form and content: monogamous versus polygamous, who has authority and different residential patterns.

4. be familiar with the deep-rooted myths about the family, including (1) families were happier in the past; (2) marrying and having children are the "natural" things to do; (3) "good" families are self-sufficient; (4) every family is a loving refuge; (5) it is possible, and we should all strive, to have a perfect marriage and to be a "perfect" family.

5. be able to distinguish between the three broad perspectives on marriage and family: the perception that the family is deteriorating; the point of view that the family is changing but not deteriorating, and the attitude that the family is stronger than ever.

6. be familiar with the changes in family that involve demographic characteristics, race, and ethnicity.

7. understand the analysis of family changes on two basic levels: macro and micro, and be familiar with the constraints that limit our choices: economic forces, technological innovations, popular culture, social movements, and family policies.

8.   appreciate the fact that a cross-cultural focus is helpful in
      understanding the American family.

CHAPTER OVERVIEW

Contemporary dramatic family arrangements are changing, but
these changes are not as they seem; some aspects of the family have
shifted, but many of the changes have been adjustments to larger
societal transformations rather than a reaction to individual preferences.

Marriage is a socially approved mating relationship with many
variations based on social norms. There are different legal forms of
marriage: ceremonial, and non-ceremonial or common-law; in modern
Western societies, marriages must not be bigamous.

The traditional definition of the family is a unit made up of two or
more people who are related by blood, marriage, or adoption, and who
live together, form an economic unit, and bear and raise children.
Academic definitions are broadening to include the growing number of
nontraditional families, including ties with fictive kin. Definitions may
become more complicated in the future.

Families have many forms and structures, but the functions that
families fulfill are very similar: legitimizing sexual activity, bearing and
raising children, providing emotional support to family members, and
establishing members' places in society.

Marriages and families vary cross-culturally; social scientists make
many distinctions, such as families of orientation and families of
procreation and extended (or consanguine) versus nuclear families.
There are different forms of marriage: monogamy, polygamy (polygyny
and polyandry), and group marriage, and because of widespread divorce
and remarriage in modern American society, we speak of serial
monogamy.

There are different patterns of authority: patriarchy, matriarchy,
and egalitarian; different residential patterns: patrilocal, matrilocal, and
neolocal; and different patterns of descent: patrilineal, matrilineal, and
bilneal.

Five of the most common myths about marriage and family are:
(1) families were happier in the past; (2) marrying and having children
are the "natural" things to do; (3) "good" families are self-sufficient; (4)
every family is always a bastion of love and support; (5) it is possible, and
we should all strive, to be a "perfect" family. Myths can be functional or

dysfunctional, or both functional and dysfunctional simultaneously. (See pages 10-14.)

There are three broad perspectives on the changing family: (1) that the family is deteriorating; (2) that the family is changing but not deteriorating; and (3) that the family is stronger than every before. Those who are extremely pessimistic about the family cite various trends to support their position: massive increase in divorces and desertions, high rates of children born out of wedlock, millions of latchkey children, large numbers of childless marriages, a decrease in the marriage rate, increasing numbers of single-parent families, and a loss of parental authority. Another group points to the fact that our contemporary family crisis has deep historical roots; that the family has been changing over time, but that this does not necessarily imply deterioration; the major problems families face are not the result of individual defects but reflect the difficulties of maintaining a family during periods of rapid change. Some evaluators argue that the family is stronger than ever; that family life today is much more loving than in the past.

Families have changed demographically, racially, and ethnically. Among the demographic changes are an increase in non-family households, a growing number of single people and cohabitants; increasing divorce and remarriage rates; larger numbers of one-parent families; more working mothers; a higher incidence of stepfamilies; and far more poverty and homelessness among American families.

There are both micro- and macro-level explanations for the changes in families, with micro perspectives commonly assuming that people have many choices, while macro perspectives focus on the constraints that limit individual options. Among the constraints are economics, technology, popular culture, social movements, and family policies.

Throughout the text, a cross-cultural perspective is employed.

CURRENT APPLICATIONS

1. Your text poses the question, "What is a family?" In some instances, this query has no particular *legal* implications: For example, some people may not regard a childless couple as a "family," but there's nothing *legal* or *illegal* about having or not having children. In many other cases, however, some confusing legal issues are involved: Should homosexual couples be permitted to legally marry? Should cohabitating couples have legal

obligations to each other, especially in the event that they terminate their relationships?

Imagine that you are a legislator who is charged with formulating policy on such issues as those just alluded to. How will you approach these perplexing questions? Think about the pros and cons of legal marriage for gay people. What do you think your constituency will say if you come out in favor of homosexual marriage?

2. As pointed out in Chapter One, some Mormon fundamentalists persist in defying state bigamy laws (and the Mormon Church, which banned polygamy in the late 1800s) by continuing to practice polygamy. Despite the fact that such violations are sometimes overlooked by state authorities due to the small number of people involved, American society still takes a very dim view of any kind of polygamy. On the other hand, there are many polygynous societies elsewhere in the world.

    If you were responsible for setting policy on the legality or illegality of polygamy, what decision would you make? Why? Do you think that most Americans are opposed to polygamy? Why is monogamy such a preferred form of marriage?

3. The author points out that myths can be dysfunctional when they result in negative (although often unintended) consequences that disrupt a family. She also notes that myths can also divert our attention from widespread social problems that create family crises.

    When Bill Cosby was asked about his popular 1980 comedy series, "The Cosby Show," spreading myths about the American family, he responded that his program was "just good clean fun." Do you think that television programming with family themes in the first decade of the 21st century is realistic? Is it stereotypical? Is it a tolerable blend of both?

    Certainly, such classic shows as "Father Knows Best," "Ozzie and Harriet," and "Leave It to Beaver" gave us hope that we can have a happy family life. "The Brady Bunch" showed viewers that blended families were certainly a viable option.

    Do you think that there are any damaging myths or functional myths associated with current or recent television series that have had a family format? Consider shows like "Roseanne," "Grace under Fire," and "Married...with Children," "Home Improvements," "Murphy Brown" (as an unwed, white, upper middle class, and successful unwed mother), and "The Simpsons" as cases in point.

4. The text discusses the debate about what is happening to the family in contemporary American society. Is it deteriorating? Is it changing, but not deteriorating? Is it stronger than ever before? Based upon your personal experiences with marriages and families, what do YOU think? Is your assessment objective and sociological, or are you allowing your own experiences to influence your thinking? Try to approach this critical analysis using a value-free stance.

KEY TERMS FILL-IN

1. A currently accepted sociological definition describes _____ as a socially approved mating relationship.

2. Culturally defined rules for behavior which help define marriage include formal laws, rituals, or religious ceremonies that specify what is acceptable and unacceptable are called social

   _____.

3. The traditional definition of the _____ is a unit made up of two or more people who are related by blood, marriage, or adoption, and who live together, form an economic unit, and bear and raise children.

4. Some states recognize nonceremonial marriages or those which are based on cohabitation as _____-_____ marriages.

5. In both ceremonial and nonceremonial marriages, the parties must meet minimal age requirements and not engage in _____ (married to a second person while the first marriage is still legal).

6. In a _____, the position of power and authority is generally held by men.

7. Cultural norms that forbid sexual intercourse between family members are called _____ _____.

8. _____ requires that people marry and/or have sexual relations within a certain group.

5

9. A child acquires the language, accumulated knowledge, attitudes, beliefs, and values of its society and culture through the process known as _____.

10. The family into which a person is born is the family of _____.

11. A family of _____ is the family a person forms later by having or adopting children.

12. A group of people who are related by marriage, blood, or adoption is known as a _____ system.

13. In much of the preindustrial world the most common family form is one in which two or more generations live together or in adjacent dwellings. This is called an _____ family.

14. One form of marriage that is allowed by society is _____ (one man, one woman).

15. A form of marriage where one man or one woman has several spouses is known as _____.

16. Because of widespread divorce and remarriage, many Americans practice _____ monogamy.

17. When a newly married couple sets up its own residence, the pattern is called a _____ one.

18. About 43 percent of the current adult U.S. population are people born between 1946 and 1964. This population cohort is commonly referred to as the _____ _____.

19. The departure from the home of grown children creates for many families the phenomena commonly referred to as the _____-_____ syndrome.

20. A _____ is made up of related and unrelated people living together in the same dwelling.

21. Small-scale patterns of social interaction in specific settings are the focus of the _____-_____ perspective.

22. The _____-_____ perspective focuses on large-scale patterns that characterize society as a whole.

6

MULTIPLE CHOICE

1. A fairly standard sociological definition describes _____ as a socially approved mating relationship.
   a. cohabitation
   b. bigamy
   c. marriage
   d. palimony

2. In both ceremonial and nonceremonial marriages, the parties must meet minimal age requirements and cannot be:
   a. patriarchal.
   b. bigamous.
   c. monogamous.
   d. neolocal.

3. The text maintains that, "any sexually expressive or parent-child relationship in which (1) people live together with a commitment, in an intimate, interpersonal relationship; (2) the members see their identity as importantly attached to the group; and (3) the group has an identity of its own" is a more inclusive definition of a:
   a. family.
   b. household.
   c. marriage.
   d. miscegenation.

4. Cultural norms that forbid sexual intercourse between family members and relatives who are too closely related to marry legally are called:
   a. exogamy rules.
   b. endogamy rules.
   c. incest taboos.
   d. polygamy taboos.

5. The family into which a person is born is the:
   a. family of orientation.
   b. family of procreation.
   c. nuclear family.
   d. kinship network.

6. In _____, one man is married to one woman.
   a. polygamy
   b. polygyny
   c. monogamy
   d. polyandry

7

7. According to anthropologist George Murdock (1967), only _____ percent of societies are strictly monogamous.
   a. 5
   b. 10
   (c.) 15
   d. 20

8. In a _____ residence the newly married couples live with the wife's consanguineal family.
   a. patrilocal
   b. neolocal
   c. geolocal
   (d.) matrilocal

9. "Only selfish people don't have children," "It's unnatural for a 25-year-old man to marry a 55-year-old woman," and "Women are natural mothers," are all myths about:
   a. the self sufficient family.
   b. naturalism.
   c. the family as a loving refuge.
   (d.) the perfect family.

10. A lack of individual responsibility, a lack of commitment to the family, and a "me-first" selfishness are some of the common reasons cited for why:
    (a.) the family is in trouble.
    b. drug use has increased.
    c. there has been an upsurge in psychiatric admissions.
    d. alcoholism has increased.

11. The estimated percentage of children who will live with a stepparent by the time they are 16 years of age is:
    a. 10 percent.
    b. 15 percent.
    (c.) 25 percent.
    d. 30 percent.

12. Which of the following is a demographic trend in families today?
    a. Fertility rates have declined.
    b. Significant shifts have occurred in the racial and ethnic composition of families.
    c. Economic transformations have had a significant impact on families.
    (d.) All of the above are demographic trends today.

13. The recent decrease in family size is due to:
    a. fewer children per family.
    b. more one-parent families.
    c. increasing age of first marriages.
    d. all of the above.

14. A _____ is made up of related and unrelated people living together in the same dwelling.
    a. family of orientation
    b. household
    c. kinship network
    d. family of procreation

15. According to the census, _____ make up one of the fastest growing groups today.
    a. married couples
    b. homosexual pairs
    c. singles
    d. serial married

16. According to the text's discussion of changes in family and non-family households:
    a. one out of every two first marriages is expected to end in divorce.
    b. one-parent families have almost tripled.
    c. almost 60 percent of all mothers with children under 1 year of age are in the labor force.
    d. all of the above

17. To study the choices people make relative to marriage and family, social scientists often take a _____ perspective.
    a. micro-level
    b. macro-level
    c. conflict
    d. functionalist

18. Which of the following is NOT a macro-level influence on the family?
    a. economic forces
    b. technological innovations
    c. individual choices
    d. popular culture

19. Popular culture includes:
    a. television.
    b. hobbies.
    c. fads.
    (d.) all of the above

20. The author of your text points out that a cross-cultural approach is employed because:
    a. no other approach is adequate.
    (b.) a traditional white, middle-class model is not adequate for understanding our marriages and families.
    c. U.S. businesses have rejected such an approach.
    d. all of the above

ANSWERS

KEY TERMS FILL-IN

ANSWERS	PAGE NUMBERS
1. marriage	2
2. norms	2
3. family	3
4. common-law marriages	2-3
5. bigamy	3
6. patriarchy	4
7. incest taboos	4
8. Endogamy	6
9. socialization	6
10. orientation	7
11. procreation	7
12. kinship	7
13. extended	7
14. monogamy	7
15. polygamy	7
16. serial	7
17. neolocal	9
18. baby boomers	18
19. empty-nest syndrome	16
20. household	17
21. micro-level	18-19
22. macro-level	18-20

MULTIPLE CHOICE

ANSWERS		PAGE NUMBERS
1.	c	2
2.	b	3
3.	a	3-4
4.	c	4
5.	a	7
6.	c	7
7.	d	7
8.	d	9
9.	b	11
10.	a	14
11.	c	18
12.	d	16-18
13.	d	16-18
14.	b	17
15.	c	17
16.	d	18
17.	a	18
18.	c	19
19.	d	20
20.	b	23

STUDYING MARRIAGE AND THE FAMILY

2

CHAPTER OBJECTIVES

Based upon their reading and careful consideration of Chapter Two, students should:

1. understand why theories and research are important in our everyday lives.

2. understand the role of theory and be familiar with the eight theoretical approaches mentioned in the text: structural functionalism, conflict, feminist, symbolic interaction, social exchange, developmental theories, and family systems theory, and be able to evaluate the strengths and weaknesses of each.

3. understand the relationship between research and social issues.

4. be familiar with the five categories of social research (survey research and focus groups, clinical research and case studies, observation, secondary analysis, and evaluation research); be able to provide examples of the various methods of each category; and be able to discuss the strengths and weaknesses of each.

5. understand the ethical and political issues associated with social science research and be able to list the guidelines for professional conduct.

CHAPTER OVERVIEW

The very words theory and research often intimidate people. Many Americans distrust quantitative data because statistics challenge comfortable beliefs and people fear that research results may perpetuate unpopular policies. Many aspects of our everyday family lives can be explained by theoretical perspectives or research. The text encourages the reader to be an "informed consumer": In order to understand marriage and family, you need to understand the most influential theories that guide social science investigation.

THEORETICAL FRAMEWORKS FOR UNDERSTANDING FAMILIES

A theory is a set of logically related statements that try to explain why a phenomenon occurs. The most influential theoretical approaches to the study of marriage and family are examined. In sociology, the ecological perspective studies the relationship and adaptation of human groups, such as families, to their physical environment. Note that ecological theory proposes that individuals' roles and environmental settings are highly interrelated. The structural-functionalist approach examines the relationship between the family and the larger society as well as the internal relationships among family members. Anything that interferes with the fulfillment of social functions is seen as dysfunctional. Functions can be both manifest-recognized or intended or latent-not recognized or intended. This approach has been criticized for being so conservative in its emphasis on order and stability and for ignoring social change.

According to conflict theories, family conflict can take many different forms. Rather than seeing change or conflict as bad or dysfunctional, conflict theorists see conflict as natural and inevitable. On a macro level, conflict theorists see society not as cooperative and stable, but as a system of inequality in which groups compete for scarce goods and services. Conflict theorists have been criticized for overemphasizing conflict and coercion at the expense of studying order, stability, and consensus.

Conflict theories provided a springboard for feminist theories (the fourth of the macro theories discussed in this section). Feminist theories include a wide range of theories including liberal feminism, radical feminism, and global feminism. They focus on the ways in which socially constructed categories of sex and gender roles shape relations between men and women in such institutions as the family, politics, and the economy. Criticisms of feminism include the fact that feminist analysis by an "old girl network" hasn't always welcomed conflicting points of view from African-American, Asian-American, Latino, Muslim, working class, or disabled women in either research or therapeutic settings. Another criticism is that most feminist research uses qualitative (rather than quantitative) methods.

Unlike structural-functionalism and conflict theories, symbolic interaction is a micro theory. Interaction is the mutual and reciprocal influencing of our behavior and attitudes; our definitions of the situation are learned through interaction with significant others; and family members play different roles. One of the most common criticisms is that because this approach emphasizes micro relationships, it ignores the impact of macro social structures.

The social-exchange theory posits that people make decisions and choices based on perceived costs and rewards and try to maximize rewards and reduce costs. Social exchange theorists argue that most decisions are based on cost-reward considerations. Exchange theorists have been accused of emphasizing the rational to the exclusion of spontaneous behavior and that it doesn't explain how rewards and costs come to be defined as such or how their values are determined.

The developmental perspective covers a very broad area and incorporates structural-functionalism, symbolic interaction, and social psychology. It examines the stages the family goes through from marriage to widowhood. These stages are called the family life cycle; as family members progress through it, they fulfill role expectations and responsibilities called developmental tasks. Developmental theories have been criticized because some critics feel that the stages are artificial; that because these theories are generally restricted to nuclear and stable families, they neglect families that take other forms; that gay and lesbian families are excluded from family life cycle theory; some critics question why life cycle theories ignore sibling relationships; and that developmental theories are not very useful in comparing family life cycles across historical periods.

The family systems theory views the family as a system, a functioning unit that solves problems, makes decisions, and achieves collective goals. The systems approach is compatible with symbolic interaction theory and is especially useful for clinicians and social workers that rely on symbolic interaction to examine the patterns of interaction among family members. Some critics argue that the family systems theory is too general to be a real theory and that it has a "sterile record."

METHODS AND TECHNIQUES IN FAMILY RESEARCH

Social scientists employ a variety of social research methods in order to study marriage and family related topics; most research comes from five major sources: surveys and focus groups, clinical research and case studies, observation, secondary analysis, and evaluation research. Surveys typically rely on questionnaires, interviews, or some combination of these techniques. Questionnaires, especially if mailed, are inexpensive and can target large numbers of respondents. Weaknesses of questionnaires include low response rates and respondent misinterpretation, leading to a self-selected sample. Interviews have the advantage of high response rates and respondent misinterpretation is

14

low, but this technique is expensive and time-consuming and respondents may be less willing to discuss sensitive issues. Telephone surveys are inexpensive, effective in obtaining representative samples, and the researcher can deal with problems as they present themselves; on the other hand, respondents are free to discontinue the interview at any time. In recent years, researchers have been using focus groups to explore issues before they engage in a large survey project; usually 6 to 12 members of a focus group participate in a guided discussion of a particular topic.

The case study or clinical-study method is the traditional approach used by those researchers who work with families on a one-to-one basis. A major strength of clinical research and case studies is that they are typically linked with long-term counseling. Weaknesses include the fact that these techniques are time-consuming and expensive and the results are not necessarily applicable to the average person or even to other troubled families.

In observation, researchers collect data by systematically observing people in their natural surroundings. In participant observation, researchers interact normally with the people they are studying but do not reveal their identities as researchers. In nonparticipant observation, researchers study phenomena without being part of the situation. Studies that use observation have the benefit of offering a deeper understanding of behavior than "one-shot" data-collection methods; they are flexible; and they do not disrupt a "natural" situation. Weaknesses include the expense involved and the fact that it may be very difficult to quantify the observations of variables, including difficulties with control.

Secondary analysis refers to the analysis of data that have been collected by someone else. This type of analysis is accessible, convenient, inexpensive, and it makes it possible to analyze longitudinal data. On the other hand, public usage may be restricted; concessions may have to be made, and the materials may be incomplete or the accuracy may be difficult to determine.

Evaluation research measures a program's effects against its goals as a means of determining its future and the future of other programs; unlike the other methods described in this chapter, evaluation research is *very applied* and has important practical applications. Evaluation research can be frustrating, however, because politics plays an important role in what is evaluated, for whom the research is done, and how the results are appraised.

Researchers are sometimes found to have plagiarized, concocted data, or outright lied. Because so much research relies on human subjects, the federal government and many other professional organizations have set up codes of ethics. Politicians are particularly distrustful of social science research, with human sexuality as one of the most sensitive research areas. Research guidelines are particularly difficult to follow when there are both ethical and political conflicts.

CURRENT APPLICATIONS

1. Place yourself in the position of a social science researcher who is contemplating a controversial investigation on the sexual behavior of America's teenagers. There has been much talk recently about the need for a nationwide survey of attitudes toward sexuality, especially in view of the AIDS epidemic. Those who are in favor of such an investigation argue that AIDS and other sexually transmitted diseases are national health menaces, and that regardless of how we may feel about our young people being sexually active, we still need to have accurate information about their sex lives.

   Obviously, there are ethical considerations here, including the rights of parents to specify whether they want their youngsters to participate in such a survey. On the other hand, if parents were given the right to exempt their children from such an investigation, how reliable would the results be? This is an excellent example of the ethical dilemma of the social scientist: the right to research versus the right of parents to restrict their children's participation.

   In contemplating your proposed investigation, how will you go about approaching such ethical considerations? What are the costs versus benefits of the research?

2. Go to the library and access the *JOURNAL OF MARRIAGE AND THE FAMILY* or the *JOURNAL OF FAMILY ISSUES*. Locate an article in this journal that deals with one of the theories of marriage and family discussed in Chapter Two. Then, describe how the authors of this article utilize this theory in approaching the topic they are researching.

3. In Chapter One, you were asked to evaluate whether you think the family is deteriorating, changing, or stronger than ever before. You

were cautioned that personal assessments can be misleading because your own experiences may not be mirrored across American society. This, of course, is one of the most important dimensions of practicing sociology: The practitioner must prevent his or her personal values from influencing the objectivity of investigations. Naturally, everybody has values and it is important for researchers to be well aware of their own points of view. Take this opportunity to examine some of your strong feelings about marriages and families. For example, do you think that only through having children can men and women *really* formulate families, or can a family exist in the absence of children? What about the number of children people should have? Do you have any biases about only children? Or, what do you think of people who divorce? Are they any different from those who stay in the same marriage for a lifetime? Why or why not? After you have had a chance to think about some of these personal points of view, go to the index of the textbook and access the discussions of these issues. How are your own points of view different from (or similar to) what we know about the entire society?

KEY TERMS FILL-IN

1. A _____ is a set of logically related statements that tries to explain why a phenomenon occurs.

2. _____-_____ theory examines the relationship between the family and the larger society.

3. According to structural-functional theory, the _____ role is held by the husband and/or father when he is the family "breadwinner."

4. Assuming the _____ role, the wife and/or mother is the homemaker, providing the emotional support and nurturing qualities that sustain the family unit and support the husband/father.

5. Functions which are recognized and/or intended and clearly evident are called _____ functions.

6. Functions which are not recognized and/or intended and are not immediately obvious are called _____ functions.

7. Although _____ theory has a long history, it became popular during the late 1960s when blacks and feminists started challenging structural-functionalism as the dominant explanation of marriage and the family.

8. _____ _____ theory is a micro-level theory that looks at the everyday behavior of individuals.

9. Our definitions of the situation are learned through interaction with people who play an important emotional role in our socialization. Symbolic interactionists refer to these people as _____ _____.

10. _____ are patterns of behavior attached to a particular status, or position in society.

11. The fundamental premise of _____ - _____ theory is that any social interaction between two people is based on the efforts of each person to maximize rewards and minimize costs.

12. Developmental theory is a _____-level perspective.

13. Developmental theories examine the many ways in which families journey through time in a series of stages, each of which focuses on different sets of events that a family goes through. This series of stages is called the family _____ _____.

14. As family members progress through the life cycle, they learn to fulfill role expectations and responsibilities such as showing affection and support for family members and socializing with people outside the family. In doing so, they are accomplishing _____ _____.

15. The _____-_____ perspective views the family as a system, a functioning unit whose daily operations and survival depend on the interactions of its members with each other and with larger social groups.

16. In _____ research, researchers systematically collect data from respondents either by questionnaire or in some form of interactive interview.

17. A _____ is any well-defined group of people about whom we want to know something specific.

18. Researchers typically draw a _____, a group of people or things that is representative of the population they wish to study.

19. In recent years, researchers have been using _____ groups to explore issues before they engage in a large survey project.

20. _____ research studies individuals or small groups of people who seek help for both physical and social problems from mental health professionals.

21. In _____ _____, researchers interact naturally with the people they are studying but frequently do not reveal their identity as researchers.

22. _____ _____ is the analysis of data that have been collected by someone else.

23. Assessment of the effectiveness of a wide variety of social programs in both the public and private sector is done by _____ research.

MULTIPLE CHOICE   ✝ 11/20

1. A _____ tries to explain logically related statements that try to explain why a phenomenon occurs.
   a. survey
   b. sample
   c. theory
   d. hypothesis

2. Micro analysts might explain teenage runaways as victims of:
   a. interpersonal family problems.
   b. peer pressure.
   c. the economy.
   d. fear of failure.

3. The _____ approach examines the relationship between the family and the larger society as well as the internal relationships among family members.
   a. unobtrusive
   b. operational
   c. social-exchange
   d. structural-functionalist

19

4. Formalization of the formation of a new family unit and the legitimization of sexual intercourse is the primary _____ function of the marriage ceremony.
   a. latent
   b. manifest
   c. operational
   (d.) developmental

5. _____ theory examines the ways in which groups disagree, struggle over power, and compete for scarce resources.
   a. Symbolic interaction
   b. Social exchange
   c. Developmental
   (d.) Conflict

6. A common misconception about feminists is that:
   a. feminists are always women or lesbians.
   b. their movement is a recent phenomena.
   c. feminists hate men.
   (d.) all of the above are common misconceptions about feminists.

7. _____ theorists argue that most decisions are based on cost-reward considerations.
   a. Structural-functionalism
   b. Conflict
   (c.) Social-exchange
   d. Symbolic-interactionist

8. As family members progress through the life cycle, they learn to fulfill role expectations and responsibilities called:
   a. social responsibilities.
   (b.) family tasks.
   c. structural functions.
   d. developmental tasks.

9. Which of the following is NOT a criticism of developmental theories?
   a. The stages of the life cycle are artificial because the processes of life are not always neatly and cleanly segmented.
   b. They neglect families that take other forms.
   c. There is too much concern with gay and lesbian families.
   (d.) That the life cycle theories ignore sibling relationships.

10. The _____ approach is especially useful for clinicians and social workers, who rely on symbolic interaction to examine the patterns of interaction among family members.
    a. conflict
    b. family-systems
    c. social-exchange
    d. token-economy

11. In _____ _____ data is systematically collected from respondents either by questionnaire or some form of interactive interview.
    a. survey research
    b. sample population
    c. cross-section
    d. population research

12. A _____ contains all of the units or elements we would ideally like to study.
    a. survey
    b. sample
    c. cross-section
    d. population

13. In a _____ sample, researchers use other criteria to collect the sample, such as convenience or the availability of respondents.
    a. probability
    b. representative
    c. nonprobability
    d. crossectional

14. Usually 6 to 12 members of a _____ participate in a guided discussion of a particular topic.
    a. survey circle
    b. clique
    c. focus group
    d. critical population

15. In _____, researchers study phenomena without being part of the situation.
    a. participant observation
    b. non-participant observation
    c. case-study method
    d. secondary analysis

16. Analysis of data that has been collected by someone else is called:
    a. secondary analysis.
    b. subordinate analysis.
    c. ancillary evaluation.
    d. surreptitious evaluation.

17. _____ research assesses the effectiveness of a wide variety of social programs, both public and private.
    a. Supplementary
    b. Secondary
    c. Evaluation
    d. Ancillary

18. Which of the following is NOT one of the basic principles of ethical family research?
    a. Researchers must avoid controversial subjects.
    b. Researchers must describe the limitations and shortcomings of their research in their published reports.
    c. Researchers must make the details of their studies and the findings available to people who request them.
    d. Researchers must obtain all subjects' consent to participate in the research.

19. Because so much research relies on human subjects, the federal government and many professional organizations have devised:
    a. numerous rules and regulations.
    b. increased numbers of forms for researchers to submit to governmental agencies.
    c. standardized guidelines.
    d. codes of ethics to protect research participants.

20. The federal government has devised a code of ethics to protect research participants that suggests that researchers:
    a. must identify the sponsors who funded the research.
    b. must make the details of their studies and the findings available to people who request them.
    c. must describe the findings and limitations of the research in their published reports.
    d. do all of the above.

ANSWERS

KEY TERMS FILL-IN

ANSWERS	PAGE NUMBERS
1. theory	28
2. Structural-functional	31
3. instrumental	31
4. expressive	31
5. manifest	31
6. latent	31
7. conflict	32
8. Symbolic interaction	33
9. significant others	33
10. Roles	33
11. social-exchange theory	34
12. micro	35
13. life cycle	35
14. developmental tasks	35
15. family-systems	35-36
16. survey	37
17. population	37
18. sample	37-38
19. focus	39
20. Clinical	40
21. participant observation	41
22. Secondary analysis	43
23. evaluation	43-44

MULTIPLE CHOICE

ANSWERS	PAGE NUMBERS
1. c	28
2. a	28
3. d	31
4. b	31
5. d	32
6. d	32
7. c	34
8. d	35

9.	c	35
10.	b	35-36
11.	a	37
12.	d	37
13.	c	38
14.	c	39
15.	b	41
16.	a	43
17.	c	43
18.	d	45
19.	d	45
20.	d	45

THE FAMILY IN HISTORICAL PERSPECTIVE

3

CHAPTER OBJECTIVES

Based upon their reading and careful consideration of Chapter Three, students should:

1. be familiar with the structure, relationships, and social class/ regional differences involving the colonial family.

2. be able to describe the various American Indian kinship systems and understand the impact of European culture on Native-American family structure.

3. be familiar with the popular misconceptions about African-American families under slavery and understand the implications of historical reconstructive efforts about the black family after emancipation.

4. understand the effects of slavery and colonization.

5. be familiar with the effects of economic exploitation on Mexican-American families, and understand that despite these hardships, how these families preserved traditional family structure, child-rearing practices, and family roles.

6. be able to discuss the impact of European immigration and the Industrial Revolution on family life, including the effects on women and children, the implications of prejudice and discrimination, and the myths associated with immigration.

7. understand how the modern family emerged from the rise of the companionate family, through the Great Depression, World War II, the Golden Fifties, and through the mid 1990s.

CHAPTER OVERVIEW

THE COLONIAL FAMILY

Historical factors play a critical role in shaping the contemporary family. The diversity that characterizes modern families has existed since colonial times. Many laws and attitudes that prevailed during the colonial period still persist today. Other aspects of the colonial family have changed considerably. In colonial times, family relations were often overseen by the community, the family was self-sufficient economically and served a variety of functions, and children were "seen and not heard." A number of predominant characteristics of the colonial family may still be observed, such as the prevalence of premarital sex, the reduced status of women's work, and social class and regional variations in family practices on the basis of socioeconomic status (in colonial times, three distinct social class divisions were evident: merchant, artisan, and laboring classes).

EARLY AMERICAN FAMILIES FROM NON-EUROPEAN CULTURES

The experiences of African-Americans and American Indians during the colonial period were varied, according to the group in question. American Indian families were extremely diverse in function, structure, sexual relations, puberty rites, and child-rearing practices. The French, Spanish, Portuguese, and British played a major role in destroying much of the American Indian culture. Within the past century, the diversity of American Indian family practices has been reduced even further through missionary activities, intrusive federal land policies, poverty on reservations, intermarriage, and federal government inducements to relocate American Indians to urban areas.

There have been numerous misinterpretations of the slave family; until the 1970s, sociologists and historians had argued that slavery had destroyed the African-American family, but more recently, researchers have shown that the family structure of slaves was not as problem-oriented and pathological as originally perceived. Contrary to past interpretations, for example, many slave households had two parents, men played important roles as fathers, and most of the women labored long and hard in the fields, rather than having a very different experience than men in the "big house." Furthermore, after emancipation, in contrast to early views that the African-American family was further disrupted by urban migration to the North, more recent analysis reveals that many of these families remained resilient despite difficult conditions.

Mexican-American families were dispossessed of their lands and colonized by European-American settlers. Despite this economic exploitation, Mexican families were very familistic and preserved their traditional family structure (e.g., *compadrazgo*), child-rearing practices, and family roles.

INDUSTRIALIZATION, URBANIZATION, AND EUROPEAN IMMIGRATION: 1820-1930

The period between 1920 and 1930 witnessed a revolution in American life and culture. European immigrants epitomized some of the most severe pressures on family life. Industrialization changed a number of family functions and altered the scope of family life. More marriages were based on love and choice rather than practical, economic considerations; parental roles within the family became more sex-segregated; and "true womanhood" came to be viewed in terms of piety, purity, submissiveness, and domesticity.

Immigration played a key role in the industrial transformation, with millions of European immigrants who worked in labor-intensive jobs at very low wages. Many of these immigrants, including large numbers of women and children, were subjected to severe social and economic discrimination, dilapidated housing conditions, and chronic health problems.

THE "MODERN" FAMILY EMERGES

By the beginning of the twentieth century, the economic, protective, recreational and religious functions of the family were being transferred to other institutions; families increasingly valued affectionate and intimate relationships and were later called the "companionate" family. From the 1920s to the golden age of the 1950s, families continued to change during the Great Depression and World War II. The Great Depression had the most devastating effects on working-class families, experiencing widespread unemployment and confinement to low-paying jobs. Families in both urban and rural areas were affected. Although the Depression was an economic disaster for many Americans, African-Americans suffered even more greatly. In many families, unemployment played havoc with gender roles. World War II had mixed effects on families; while many women (especially African-American mothers) finally found reasonably well paying jobs, many families were disrupted by death, divorce, and incompatibility.

After World War II, when women were no longer needed in the workplace and returning veterans needed jobs, the propaganda about family roles changed almost overnight. The "Golden Fifties" saw the family roles of white, middle-class women relegated to full-time nurturance of children and husbands. Husbands' roles were largely confined to work. Family togetherness and suburban living were emphasized.

Since the 1960s, family functions and structure have changed considerably. In the 1970s, families had lower birth rates, higher divorce rates, and larger numbers of women entered colleges and graduate programs. In the 1980s, more people over 25 years of age postponed marriage, and many of those already married delayed having children. Out-of-wedlock births, especially among teenage girls and one-parent families, increased significantly. There was also a burgeoning of two–income families and adult children who lived at home with their parents due to financial difficulties during the 1980s.

Economic problems would become more severe during the 1990s. Increased racial and ethnic diversity coupled with economic downturns would increase anxiety among whites and some responded with violent racist attacks.

CURRENT APPLICATIONS

1.   Consider how the traditional/stereotypic image of family life in the colonial period is still romanticized today in the media. List some examples of how Americans are led to regard family life in history as "better." How do the media fit in with these widespread images of family? Contrast this "classical family of Western nostalgia" with reality. What contemporary television programs that you have watched mirror some of these romanticized images of marriages and families?

2.   It is generally recognized that a spirit of "familism" prevailed in the colonial period and continued up until the industrial revolution. This "familistic" orientation prescribed that individual well being took a back seat to the family's welfare as a whole. As industrialism grew, this trend was replaced with a spirit of "individualism," where young people began to make decisions based upon their own self-interest (e.g., career choice, whether to marry or not, etc.). Think about how your life would be affected if certain personal decisions you have come to take for granted were regarded as less important than how each of these choices would affect your family.

3. The key to understanding family variation lies in the many ties that families have to community and society. These ties account for the tremendous family diversity that we see today in American society. Think about how immigration created an almost infinite rainbow of values, customs, and lifestyles in America. Furthermore, concentrate on how an appreciation of this diversity is essential to an accurate interpretation of contemporary family life.

4. Many social observers have remarked that the outcome of the O.J. Simpson trial serves as a stark reminder of the degree of racial separation which is still present in this country. What do you think the future holds for relationships between the members of different racial and ethnic groups in American society? Do you think that interracial and interethnic marriages will become more commonplace or will they become less common? What are your feelings about what *should* happen?

KEY TERMS FILL-IN

1. In colonial times, the New England custom in which a young man and woman, both fully dressed, spent the night in bed together, separated by a wooden board was called _____.

2. In Mexican society, family relations took priority over individual well-being and was referred to as _____.

3. A key factor in conserving Mexican culture was the concept and practice of _____, in which close relationships were established and maintained among parents, children, and children's godparents.

4. In Mexican society, masculinity was expressed through _____, which stresses such male attributes as dominance, assertiveness, pride and sexual prowess.

5. Between 1820 and 1860, women's magazines and religious literature referred to attributes of _____ _____ (women being judged as "good" if they displayed the virtues of piety, submissiveness, purity, and domesticity).

MULTIPLE CHOICE

1. The _____ family was the prevalent form in both England and in the first settlements in America.
    (a.) extended
    b. nuclear
    c. three-generation
    d. five-generation

2. In the 1670s, the Massachusetts General Court directed towns to appoint _____ to oversee every 10 or 12 households to ensure that marital relations were harmonious and that parents disciplined unruly children.
    a. artisans
    b. barristers
    (c.) apprentices
    d. tithingmen

3. In the Puritan community, the two primary sexual offenses were adultery and illegitimacy. Both were condemned because they:
    (a.) threatened the family structure.
    b. weakened the control of the church.
    c. showed disrespect for parental authority.
    d. increased the need for social welfare.

4. In Colonial America, _____ was recognized as a problem, but not one serious enough to warrant a divorce.
    a. desertion
    b. bigamy
    c. incompatibility
    (d.) impotence

5. In Colonial America between _____ percent of all children died before their first birthday.
    a. 5 and 10
    b. 10 and 30
    (c.) 15 and 40
    d. 25 and 50

6. The Puritans believed that children were born:
    (a.) pure.
    b. miniature adults.
    c. with original sin and were inherently stubborn, willful, and selfish.
    d. as a blank page to be molded by their parents.

30

7. In the _____ class, the patriarchs typically were shipping and commercial entrepreneurs.
    a. merchant
    b. underclass
    c. laboring
    d. artisan

8. The _____ class was characterized by highly skilled occupations.
    a. merchant
    b. underclass
    c. laboring
    d. artisan

9. The _____ class was made up mainly of migrants in the community.
    a. merchant
    b. underclass
    c. laboring
    d. artisan

10. In Indian societies in North America, _____ had class structures that often included slaves at the bottom; they were polygynous, and lived in elaborate houses.
    a. chiefdoms
    b. tribes
    c. bands
    d. clans

11. _____ occurred in more than 20 percent of the marriages among Indians of the Great Plains.
    a. Monogamy
    b. Abstinence
    c. Celibacy
    d. Polygyny

12. In most Indian societies, _____ was/were more elaborate for girls than for boys.
    a. formal education
    b. puberty rites
    c. sexual regulation
    d. adolescence

13. The first African Americans in the English North American colonies were brought over as:

a. slaves.
b. indentured servants.
c. freeman.
d. immigrants.

14. Studies of slave families in Mississippi, Tennessee and Louisiana indicate that between _____ percent of marriages were terminated for economic reasons.
a. 5 to 15
b. 20 to 30
c. 35 to 40
d. 50 to 60

15. Most of the female slaves over _____ years of age worked in the field, sunup to sundown, 6 days per week.
a. 10
b. 15
c. 18
d. 21

16. Mexican migrants were assigned to particular jobs by:
a. gender.
b. age.
c. education.
d. skill level.

17. In Mexican families, _____ took priority over individual well-being.
a. community needs
b. religious activities
c. family relations
d. peer group relations

18. In Mexican society, masculinity was expressed through:
a. compadrazgo.
b. artistic ability.
c. religious activity.
d. machismo.

19. The turn of the century saw married couples increasingly stressing the importance of sexual attraction and compatibility in their relationships which contributed to the rise of the _____ family.
    a. intrinsic
    b. companionate
    c. intuitive
    d. natural

20. The Depression had the most devastating effect on:
    a. the poor – the working class.
    b. the middle class.
    c. the upper class.
    d. The Depression had an equally devastating effect on all social classes in the U.S.

21. Because of _____, World War II was the only time when even working-class women were praised for working outside the home.
    a. food rationing
    b. gasoline rationing
    c. the labor shortage
    d. the currency shortage

22. Which of the following is true about the "Golden Fifties"?
    a. Women were needed in the workplace more than ever before.
    b. The return of fathers at the end of the war had a very unsettling effect for many American children.
    c. There was a hesitancy on the part of most Americans to move from cities to the suburbs.
    d. The consumption of drugs was almost nonexistent among American men and women.

23. According to the text's discussion of the family since the 1960s,
    a. in the 1970s, families had higher birth rates, lower divorce rates, and smaller numbers of women entered colleges and graduate programs.
    b. in the 1980s, fewer people over 25 years of age postponed marriage.
    c. out-of-wedlock births among teenage girls increased precipitously during the late 1990s.
    d. two-income families and adult children who continued to live at home with their parents because of financial difficulties became more widespread during the 1990s.

ANSWERS

KEY TERMS FILL-IN

ANSWERS		PAGE NUMBER
1.	bundling	51
2.	familism	60
3.	compadrazgo	60
4.	machismo	60
5.	true womanhood	61

MULTIPLE CHOICE

ANSWERS		PAGE NUMBER
1.	b	50
2.	d	50
3.	a	51
4.	c	52
5.	b	52
6.	c	52
7.	a	54
8.	d	54
9.	c	54
10.	a	54
11.	d	54
12.	b	56
13.	b	56
14.	c	57-58
15.	a	58
16.	a	59
17.	c	60
18.	d	60
19.	b	65
20.	a	66
21.	c	67
22.	b	68
23.	d	69

GENDER ROLES AND SOCIALIZATION

CHAPTER OBJECTIVES

Based upon their reading and careful consideration of Chapter Four, students should:

1. be able to distinguish between sex and gender and to define gender roles.

2. be familiar with the nature-nurture debate as this controversy relates to gender roles for men and women in society.

3. be able to discuss the three main theories of socialization: social-learning theory, cognitive-development theory, and gender schema theory.

4. be able to identify the four primary sources of socialization for children: parents; toys, play, and peers; teachers and schools; and popular culture and the media; and be prepared to discuss how each of these socializing agents influences the formation of gender identities.

5. understand traditional views of gender roles.

6. understand the implications of gender roles in adulthood, in higher education, in marriage and household work, in the workplace, and in terms of language and communication.

7. understand current gender-role changes and constraints.

8. be able to analyze why people are frequently ambivalent about change and understand how androgyny may be a possible alternative to traditional gender roles.

9. be familiar with cross-cultural differences in gender role identity and be able to provide examples of male-dominated, progressive, and middle societies.

CHAPTER OVERVIEW

GENDER MYTHS AND BIOLOGICAL PUZZLES

Men and women are perceived and treated differently. The terms "sex," "gender," and "gender roles" are differentiated in the social sciences. Sex refers to the ascribed biological characteristics while gender refers to the socially learned behaviors and expectations associated with our physiological sex. Like other roles, gender roles are learned, and the expected behavior can vary depending upon the situation. Much of people's self concepts reflect gender expectations.

The debate rages on as to whether gender roles are a reflection of nature (biology) or nurture (environment). Those who believe that nature is more important than nurture argue that there are innate differences between men and women. Although most social scientists acknowledge that biology is important, there is little evidence that women are naturally better parents, that men are naturally more aggressive, or that men and women are inherently different. Scientists believe that many of the existing differences between men and women are due to hormonal secretions. Indeed, research on transsexuals, hermaphrodites, and gender reassignment challenges the widespread belief that men and women are different socially because they have different sexual organs. An emphasis on gender differences overlooks the importance of the social context in which women and men live.

HOW WE LEARN GENDER ROLES

There is no comprehensive theory of gender-role learning. The major socialization theories focus on early learning processes. Three perspectives are typically used to explain how gender roles are learned. The central notion in social-learning theory is that both children and adults learn gender-appropriate roles not through psychosexual development but through the environment. From this perspective, gender roles are learned through rewards and punishments, instruction, and role modeling. Cognitive-development theory, based largely on the work of Jean Piaget and Lawrence Kohlberg, assumes that children are actively involved in learning all behavior, including gender identity. Whether young children learn rigid or egalitarian gender-role concepts depends upon which concepts are endorsed by society. Carol Gilligan argues that Kohlberg's thesis emphasized only men's development, and proposes a different sequence for women. According to Gilligan, men attach greater priority to formal rights and competition while women value caring relationships and cooperative interaction. A newer perspective that incorporates elements of cognitive development theory is the gender schema theory. This theory focuses on how children actively construct for themselves what it means to be male or female. Children use gender schema to evaluate the behavior of others as gender appropriate ("good") or gender inappropriate ("bad"). Gender schema may become more rigid during adolescence, when young people frequently feel compelled to conform to peers gender-role stereotypes. They may become more flexible again during adulthood. Social learning theory, cognitive development theory, and gender schema theory are often used together. "One perspective is not better than the other, just different" according to Benokraitis.

WHO TEACHES GENDER ROLES?

Gender expectations are acquired from different sources such as parents; toys, play, and peer interaction; teachers and schools; and popular culture and the media. Research shows that parents treat their male and female children differently and that sex-differentiated expectations continue through childhood and into adolescence. Girls and boys typically play with different types of toys. This gives them different messages about gender roles. Therefore they generally play differently; girls tend to play alone or one-on-one. Girls usually play cooperative, repetitive games with simple rules. Boys are more likely to play in teams, to interact more, are more competitive, and play more complex and elaborate games. Teachers often treat boys and girls differently in the classroom. Research shows that boys receive more attention and that girls are not expected to find "answers" for themselves. Most of the studies of children's books and textbooks conclude that women are not visible, and when they are depicted, they are not as important as men. Popular culture and the media are also extremely influential in sending messages about gender roles. The extent to which the media reinforces sex stereotyping can be observed in advertising, magazines, and in television.

TRADITIONAL VIEWS AND GENDER ROLES

Traditional gender roles are based on the belief that women should fulfill expressive (socioemotional) functions, whereas men should play instrumental (task-oriented) roles. The traditional male is a "superman": tough, hard, and self-controlled. The traditional woman, on the other hand, is nurturant, dependent and submissive.

Traditional gender roles have both positive and negative consequences, advantages and disadvantages. On the positive side, traditional gender roles promote stability, continuity, and predictability-- men and women know what is expected of them. On the negative side, traditional gender roles can create stress, boredom, and anxiety. That they probably never characterized the lives of real men and women is one of the biggest problems with traditional gender roles.

CONTEMPORARY GENDER ROLES IN ADULTHOOD

Many of us believe that adults have more options than ever before to "do gender" any way they want. Certainly, there have been many changes, especially in women's roles.

Because many mothers work outside the home today, there is more pressure on fathers to share in child rearing and housework. Men today have "permission" that they didn't have a generation ago to care for their children. In most cases, one of the major sources of tension is that many fathers do not participate in the "second shift." While there has been progress, many gender roles in the workplace affect both men and women negatively. There continues to be some sex discrimination in the workplace, but recent legislation involving sexual harassment has brought greater sensitivity to these issues.

As consumers, women routinely pay more and get less as consumers in everyday transactions.

By adulthood, men and women communicate very differently, both verbally and nonverbally. Research demonstrates that women's communication is a reaction to their submissive position. They use more intensifiers, hedges, qualifiers, disclaimers, verbal fillers and verbal fluencies. Men's communication reflects their dominant position. These language differences "keep women in their place."

CURRENT GENDER ROLE CHANGES AND CONSTRAINTS

There is a great deal of ambivalence about changing gender roles and the egalitarian attitudes that are becoming more pervasive. Men and women organize their lives according to different "temporal modes," and breaking out of the traditional gender roles can be unsettling. In terms of sexual equality, there is tremendous variation cross-culturally.

A GLOBAL VIEW: VARIATIONS IN GENDER ROLES

Many societies are male dominated, but there are others that are more progressive than the United States in terms of egalitarianism. Societies are placed on a continuum —at one end of the continuum are many societies, primarily in the Middle East and developing countries, where most women are almost totally dominated by men; at the other end of the gender-role continuum are those societies like France and

Sweden that are considered more progressive than the U.S. Other societies (e.g. Japan) are in the middle of the continuum.

IS ANDROGYNY THE ANSWER?

A discussion of androgyny suggests that a blend of male and female roles may be the solution to sexist attitudes toward love, sex, and marriage.

CURRENT APPLICATIONS

1. In discussing communication between the sexes, the text makes reference to Deborah Tannen's book, *You Just Don't Understand* (1990). Ms. Tannen presents convincing data which demonstrates that men and women have great difficulty communicating with each other due to differences in their socialization. Step into the role of "participant observer" the next time you have an opportunity to listen to men and women conversing. You might do this at a social gathering or perhaps in small group interactions that you have on a daily basis. Pay special attention to miscommunication between the men and women you are observing. Try to evaluate <u>why</u> these people are having trouble communicating with each other.

2. A very controversial topic in the news these days is that of *comparable worth*. Social critics have called attention to these inequities as prime examples of sexual discrimination in the work place. Engage your friends in conversation about the issue of comparable worth. Ask them to vocalize how much they earn doing various types of work. Look for examples of inequity on the basis of sex. Then ask these people to express how they feel about it...chances are, the women will be actively interested in changing the situation; the men, on the other hand, may be more complacent.

3. Evaluate the extent to which men and women are represented on the faculty at your college or university. You can do this by consulting a current issue of the school bulletin or by contacting the office of institutional research. Which disciplines have larger proportions of women? Interview people in those fields to find out why. Is there any evidence that your school discriminates against either women or men in hiring practices? Be sure to ask the people you talk to if steps have been taken in the recent past to achieve equality in these areas.

KEY TERMS FILL-IN

1. _____ is the group of biological characteristics with which we are born.

2. _____ refers to learned attitudes and behaviors that characterize people of one sex or the other.

3. _____ roles are distinctive patterns of attitudes, behaviors, and activities that society prescribes for females and males.

4. _____ are chemical substances that are secreted into the bloodstream by the endocrine glands.

5. _____ are people who feel that their gender identity is out of sync with their anatomical sex.

6. _____ _____ refers to a person's emotional and intellectual awareness of being either male or female.

7. _____, also known as intersexuals, are people born with both male and female sex organs (internal and/or external).

8. The central notion of _____-_____ theory is that both children and adults learn gender appropriate roles not through psychosexual development, but through the environment.

9. _____-_____ theory views learning as an active process in which children interact with their environment and using the mental processes of thinking, understand, reason, interpret and apply the information they have gathered.

10. _____ _____ theory focuses on how male and female newborns become conventionally masculine and feminine adults.

11. _____ _____ is any unwelcome sexual advance, request for sexual favors, or other conduct of a sexual nature that makes a person uncomfortable and interferes with his or her work.

12. _____ _____ refers to the frustration and uncertainties experienced by a person who is confronted with the

requirements of two or more roles that are incompatible with each other.

13. In _____, both culturally defined masculine and feminine characteristics are blended within the same person.

MULTIPLE CHOICE

1. We are born male or female but we learn the psychological aspects associated with:
   a. gender.
   b. sex.
   c. norms.
   e. values.

2. _____ shape our lives at work, at home, and in social groups.
   a. Sex roles
   b. Normative behaviors
   c. Gender expectations
   d. Gender roles

3. Hormones are chemical substances that are secreted into the bloodstream by the:
   a. spleen.
   b. thyroid.
   c. endocrine glands.
   d. lymph glands.

4. The dominant female hormone is:
   a. estrogen.
   b. progesterone.
   c. testosterone.
   d. premarin.

5. _____ typically corresponds to a person's biological sex characteristics.
   a. Sex role
   b. Gender reassignment
   c. Gender identity
   d. Transsexualism

6. People who feel that their gender identity is out of sync with their anatomical sex are referred to as:
   a. transsexuals.

b. homosexuals.

c. heterosexuals.

d. hermaphrodites.

7. Patriarchal societies are:
   a. egalitarian.
   b. dominated by males.
   c. dominated by females.
   d. characterized by a democratic ideal.

8. People who are born with both male and female sex organs are referred to as:
   a. transsexuals.
   b. homosexuals.
   c. heterosexuals.
   d. hermaphrodites.

9. According to _____ theory, children learn gender roles through imitation or role modeling of same-sex significant others.
   a. Freudian
   b. identification
   c. social-learning
   d. cognitive-development

10. According to _____ theory, gender-appropriate roles are learned through interaction with the environment.
    a. social-learning
    b. cognitive-development
    c. identification
    d. modeling

11. _____ is based largely on the work of Jean Piaget and Lawrence Kohlberg.
    a. Social-learning
    b. Cognitive-development
    c. Identification
    d. Modeling

12. Children use _____ to evaluate the behavior of others as gender appropriate or gender inappropriate.
    a. modeling
    b. gender schema
    c. identification
    d. social-learning

13. Which of the following is true about parents' effect on their children learning gender roles?
    a. Parents are no longer influential sources of learning about sex roles.
    b. Parents communicate differently with boys and girls, starting at an early age.
    c. Parents tend to discontinue promoting self-stereotypical behavior once their children begin school.
    d. Parents' sex-typed socialization of their children is very different from what children learn when exposed to the larger culture.

14. A study conducted by Kimmel and Messner (1995) revealed that young black males who are especially vulnerable to experiencing daily racism and inequality may establish their male identity through:
    a. "cool pose."
    b. higher education.
    c. participation in sports.
    d. frequent sexual activity.

15. Research on the role of toys, play, and peer interaction on gender roles shows that:
    a. boys are still more likely than girls to participate in warlike games and sports.
    b. boys and girls often play differently.
    c. boys' toys – including educational video games – encourage competition and following strict rules; girls' toys foster nurturance and emotional expressiveness.
    d. all of the above are true statements.

16. Studies of gender-role socialization in schools indicates that:
    a. teachers often treat boys and girls differently in the classroom.
    b. girls are given more time to talk in class, are called on more often, and are given more positive feedback.
    c. sex-stereotyping has all but disappeared among high school guidance counselors.
    d. none of the above are true.

17. Any unwelcome sexual advance, request for sexual favors, or other conduct of a sexual nature, which makes a person uncomfortable or interferes with his or her work is known as:
    a. racial harassment.
    b. racial discrimination.
    c. sexual discrimination.
    d. sexual harassment.

18. Sexual harassment in the workplace had a low-profile until:
    a. the 1986 Supreme Court decision, *Mentor Savings Bank v. Venson*.
    b. Anita Hills' testimony during the 1991 Senate confirmation hearings of Clarence Thomas' Supreme Court judge candidacy.
    c. charges of sexual misconduct by drill instructors at Aberdeen Proving Ground in Maryland.
    d. the "Tailhook Scandal" that charged harassment by U.S. Navy officers.

19. An exception to women's paying more as consumers is in:
    a. automotive insurance.
    b. car repair charges.
    c. dry cleaning costs.
    d. beauty shop charges for a basic shampoo, cut, and blow-dry.

20. According to Deborah Tannen (1990), women are most likely to use "_____-talk," a way of establishing connections and negotiating relationships.
    a. report
    b. rap
    c. rapport
    d. narrative

21. In _____, both culturally defined masculine and feminine characteristics are blended within the same person.
    a. polygamy
    b. androgyny
    c. multiplicity
    d. polygyny

22. In India, most women are under the authority of fathers, brothers, husbands, or husbands' families and are often considered property epitomized by the:
    a. dowry.
    b. bride's gift.
    c. nadle.
    d. dowager.

ANSWERS

KEY TERMS FILL-IN

ANSWERS	PAGE NUMBERS
1. Sex	73
2. Gender	74
3. Gender	74
4. Hormones	75
5. Transsexuals	75
6. Gender identity	75
7. Hermaphrodites	79
8. social-learning	80
9. Cognitive-development	80-81
10. Gender schema	81
11. Sexual harassment	97
12. Role conflict	99
13. androgyny	100

MULTIPLE CHOICE

ANSWERS	PAGE NUMBERS
1. a	74
2. d	74

3.	c	75
4.	a	75
5.	c	75
6.	a	75
7.	b	77
8.	d	79
9.	c	80
10.	a	80
11.	b	80-81
12.	b	81
13.	b	82-83
14.	a	83
15.	d	83-84
16.	a	84-85
17.	d	97
18.	b	97
19.	a	98
20.	c	98-99
21.	b	100
22.	a	101

5

LOVE AND LOVING RELATIONSHIPS

CHAPTER OBJECTIVES

Based upon their reading and careful consideration of Chapter Five, students should:

1. understand the importance of love, both as a feeling and a behavior.

2. understand the connections among caring, commitment, and intimacy.

3. be familiar with the differences among biological, psychological, and sociological theories of love.

4. be prepared to discuss the major theories of love: attachment theory, Reiss's wheel theory, and Sternberg's triangular theory.

5. be able to identify Lee's six styles of loving and provide a description of each.

6. be familiar with the functions of love and loving.

7. be able to characterize romantic love and discuss why it tends to die and what happens afterward.

8. be familiar with gender and sexual orientation differences concerning love and society's attitudes toward same sex love.

9. understand the barriers to experiencing love, including the implications of jealousy and other types of controlling behavior, including guilt-trips and emotional and physical abuse.

10. be familiar with the connection between romantic love and long-term love.

CHAPTER OVERVIEW

Love, both as a feeling and a behavior, is essential for human survival; it nourishes us physically, socially, and emotionally. Love for oneself, or self-love, is also essential; it is a prerequisite for loving others.

WHAT IS LOVE?

Love is an elusive concept and complex phenomenon. Definitions of love vary across different social contexts. Both micro-and macro-level variables are responsible for the development of love, but it is generally agreed that respect and caring are the common denominators of loving relationships. It is important to differentiate among sexual arousal (or lust), sexual desire, and love, especially romantic love.

CARING, INTIMACY, AND COMMITMENT

For love to survive, key words are caring, intimacy, commitment, and change. Many concepts of love include caring. All definitions of intimacy emphasize feelings of closeness. Commitment refers to a person's intention to remain in a relationship no matter what happens.

There are numerous theories of love; none of these is definitive, but all of these perspectives help us to understand the various dimensions of love. Most of the "theories" are really *typologies*, or classification systems that focus on courtship rather than love. Biological perspectives maintain that love is founded in evolution, biology, and chemistry. Psychological and sociological perspectives claim that culture is responsible for expressions of love. Attachment theory posits that our primary motivation in life is to be connected with other people. Despite the popularity of attachment theory, there are some serious flaws. Reiss's wheel theory of love involves four stages: rapport, self-revelation, mutual dependency, and personality need fulfillment. Borland extended Reiss's wheel theory by examining love relationships as "clocksprings;" his notion of a coiled spring that winds and unwinds provided more flexibility to the wheel theory. Sternberg's triangular theory of love emphasizes the components of love in terms of three elements of a triangle: intimacy, passion, and decision/commitment. Lee has derived six basic styles of loving: eros (love of beauty and the root of the word "erotic"), mania (madness), ludus (carefree and casual), storge (affectionate love), agape (self-giving love), and pragma (practical love); these are ideal constructs, and in real life, the styles of loving overlap and vary in intensity.

FUNCTIONS OF LOVE AND LOVING

Love fulfills many functions; some are positive in that they help to maintain societies; others are dysfunctional because they threaten a species' existence and peaceful relations on an individual, group, or societal level. The positive functions of love include survival, improving longevity and the quality of life, control, inspiration, fun, and lust.

EXPERIENCING LOVE

There are important gender and sexual orientation differences in terms of love; contrary to popular belief, men are more romantic than women, but they are also less intimate. Showing love also depends on attitudes about gender roles. Heterosexual and same-sex love are very similar; one of the biggest differences is that lesbians and gay men cannot show their affection in public.

There are many micro-level and macro-level barriers to love; most people have internalized a variety of myths about love, which can be stifling. Mass society detracts from personal, face-to-face interaction. Although traditional sex roles have begun to break down, there is still a great deal of social inequality between men and women, including the double standard, and this inequality impedes the development of love. Our cultural values encourage individualism and this atmosphere leads to a preoccupation with self. Most societies exert control over love through the norms and values that are internalized in the family. In general, society not only disapproves of homosexual behavior and unions but sees homosexual couples as less in love and less satisfied in comparison with heterosexual couples. Sometimes personality traits or family history get in the way of finding love. Any number of obstacles can impede our way to love. Some are micro-level, such as the impersonality of mass society, demographic variables, our culture's double standard for men and women, and its emphasis on individualism. Other barriers are micro-level, such as certain kinds of personality characteristics and family experiences.

WHEN LOVE GOES WRONG

People sometimes assume that jealousy is a healthy sign of love. On the contrary, jealousy is destructive and controlling. Jealousy seems to have an adverse effect on love. Some jealous lovers become obsessed; in recent years, *stalking* by a jealous lover has been recognized as a serious problem. Jealousy is not universal, but it is widespread. Jealously is not the only type of unhealthy, controlling behavior in love relationships. Threatening the withdrawal of love or inducing feelings of guilt can be deeply distressing to a partner; inflicting severe emotional and physical abuse can be devastating.

HOW COUPLES CHANGE: ROMANTIC AND LONG-TERM LOVE

Romantic love can be both exhilarating and disappointing. It is long term love, however, that provides security and constancy. Tennov's list of characteristics of romantic love portray romantic love as idealized, emotional, passionate, and melodramatic; it is a phenomenon that thrives on two beliefs - love at first sight and fate.

Many characteristics of romantic love overlap those of long-term love (some combination of eros, ludus, long-term storge, agape, and pragma). Key differences, however, are that romantic love is simple whereas lasting love is more complicated; also, romantic love is self-centered, whereas long-term love is altruistic. It is also noted that it is easier to fall in love than to stay in love. There is no one formula for sustaining a long-term relationship. Many variables play a role in maintaining love.

A GLOBAL VIEW

A look at love in other countries and cultures reveal many variations. Anthropologists have found evidence of romantic love in most of the cultures they have studied and conclude that romantic love constitutes a near-universal phenomenon. Evidence indicates that attitudes toward love may also vary by gender from one country to another.

CURRENT APPLICATIONS

1.   On page 108 of your text, an *Ask Yourself* boxed insert provides a brief quiz entitled, "How Much Do You Know about Love?" Even if you have already taken the quiz, go back and run through it again. This time, concentrate on whether your previous confidence in any of these myths has affected your behavior in a (presumably) love-based relationship. Try to be as objective as you can in your personal assessment. Has your faith in these myths caused you any difficulties? How?

2.   Take a trip to your local newsstand and examine the latest issues of magazines like *Cosmoplitan* and *Redbook*. Chances are, there will be several articles in these publications that concentrate on love-related topics. Most of the time, *love* and *sex* are blurred

together and sometimes indistinguishable. You may observe a "pattern" to the focus of these writings: What to Do When the Thrill Is Gone," "How to Make Sure He Doesn't Stray," or You Say You Just Don't Talk Anymore?" Magazines like these are extremely popular in American society, and articles such as those just referenced keep appearing again and again...the titles have changed but the topic is still the same. Americans spend a lot of time worrying about their "love-lives." Read a few of the articles in these publications. What does their content tell us about Americans' attitudes toward love?

3. Your text discusses *jealousy* as one of the major obstacles to love. Many people tend to interpret the implications of jealousy exclusively in terms of opposite sex relationships. In fact, jealousy can involve same-sex friendships or even inanimate objects. For example, a woman could be jealous of her husband spending a lot of time with his best male friend; a man might well be threatened by his wife's strong interest in attending a graduate school. Form a small group in your class or among your close friends in order to discuss your respective experiences with jealousy. Concentrate on how such feelings detract from the expression of love, respect, caring, etc.

4. The text points out that contrary to popular belief, men are more romantic than women but that men are less intimate. These observations reflect important gender differences with respect to love. Current research helps us to understand some of the reasons for these differences. Proceeding from what we know from these investigations, apply this knowledge to your personal experiences. Ask yourself a series of questions: What elements are most important in terms of your experiencing feelings of love for another person? If you are male, do you think that you "fall in love" quickly or gradually? If you are female, concentrate on the importance of intimacy in a relationship.

KEY TERMS FILL-IN

1. _____-_____ refers to open communication where one person offers his or her honest thoughts and feelings to another person in hope that truly open communication will follow.

2. _____ refers to a person's intention to remain in a relationship no matter what happens.

3. According to _____ theory, "our primary motivation in life is to be connected with other people—because it is the only security we ever have. Maintaining closeness is a bona fide survival need."

4. _____ is love of beauty and is the root of the word "erotic."

5. _____ may also find expression in anxiety, sleeplessness, fever, loss of appetite, and headaches.

6. _____ is carefree and casual love that is considered "fun and games."

7. _____ is a slow-burning, peaceful, and affectionate love that "just comes naturally."

8. According to the text, the classical Christian view of love is known as _____.

9. _____ can be described as "love with a shopping list."

MULTIPLE CHOICE

1. The willingness to please and accommodate the other, acceptance of the other person's faults and shortcomings, and as much concern about the loved one's welfare as one's own are three elements Safilios-Rothschild posits as necessary for:
   a.   a woman to be classified as a "true woman."
   b.   a man to be classified as a "true man."
   c.   motherhood.
   d.   a valid love relationship.

2. The _____ theory posits that "our primary motivation in life is to be connected with other people because it is the only security we ever had."
   a.   attachment
   b.   Ainsworth
   c.   commitment
   d.   bonding

3. According to a study by Cindy Hazan and her associates, adults who had a tendency to fall in love easily and wanted a commitment almost immediately are:
   a. anxious/ambivalent.
   b. avoidant.
   c. self-possessed.
   d. secure.

4. _____ perspectives maintain that love is founded in evolution, biology, and chemistry.
   a. Biological
   b. Environmental
   c. Psychological
   d. Sociological

5. Rapport, self-revelation, mutual dependency, and personality need fulfillment are the four stages of Reiss's _____ theory of love.
   a. complementary needs
   b. clockspring alternatives
   c. triangular
   d. wheel

6. In the _____ theory of love, Borland suggested relationships might end abruptly if they are so tightly overwound that they cannot grow.
   a. complementary needs
   b. clockspring alternatives
   c. triangular
   d. wheel

7. Intimacy, passion, and decision/commitment are the components of Sternberg's _____ theory of love.
   a. complementary needs
   b. clockspring alternatives
   c. triangular
   d. wheel

8. _____ epitomizes "love at first sight."
   a. Storge
   b. Ludus
   c. Eros
   d. Mania

9. _____ lovers are consumed by thoughts of the beloved.
   a. Storgic
   b. Ludic
   c. Erotic
   d. Manic

10. Because a _____ lover does not want a commitment, sex is typically self-centered and may be exploitative.
    a. storgic
    b. ludic
    c. erotic
    d. manic

11. _____ is characterized by a lack of ecstasy and a lack of despair.
    a. Storge
    b. Ludus
    c. Eros
    d. Mania

12. _____ is altruistic, self-sacrificing, and directed toward all humankind.
    a. Pragma
    b. Erotomania
    c. Ludus
    d. Agape

13. According to the triangular theory, love can vary in its mix of:
    a. intimacy.
    b. passion.
    c. commitment.
    d. all of the above.

14. Sternberg calls a relationship that is committed but neither intimate nor passionate a(n) _____ relationship.
    a. companionate
    b. empty
    c. transitory
    d. emergent

15. The biological perspective of love contends that love that endures beyond the first few months is due to the effect of:
    a.   PEA
    b.   phermones
    c.   endorphins
    d.   neurocarbons

16. Comparisons of men and women in love indicate that:
    a.   men often fall in love faster than women.
    b.   for most men and women, they agree that trust and respect are central to love.
    c.   although men may be more romantic than women and the sexes may show their affection differently, there are probably more similarities than differences between the love attitudes of women and men.
    d.   all of the above are true statements.

17. Studies of jealousy indicate that:
    a.   jealousy is a universal trait.
    b.   twice as many women as men worry more about sexual infidelity than emotional infidelity.
    c.   jealousy is usually an unhealthy manifestation of insecurity.
    d.   all of the above are true statements.

18. In societies like India, _____ is not necessarily a prerequisite for marriage.
    a.   love
    b.   intelligence
    c.   wealth
    d.   physical attractiveness

19. Anthropologists William Jankowiak and Edward Fischer (1992) found evidence of romantic love in _____ percent of the 166 cultures they studied and concluded that romantic love is not a product of Western culture.
    a.   27
    b.   56
    c.   89
    d.   97

20. Romantic love is:
    a.   idealized.
    b.   emotional.
    c.   passionate
    d.   all of the above.

ANSWERS

KEY TERMS FILL-IN

ANSWERS	PAGE NUMBERS
1. Self-disclosure	109
2. Commitment	109
3. attachment	111
4. Eros	114
5. Mania	114
6. Ludus	114-115
7. Storge	115
8. agape	115
9. Pragma	115

MULTIPLE CHOICE

ANSWERS	PAGE NUMBERS
1. d.	107
2. a	111
3. a	111-112
4. a	110
5. d	112-113
6. b	113
7. c	113
8. c	114
9. d	114
10. b	114-115
11. a	115
12. d	115
13. d	113
14. b	114
15. c	110-111
16. d	117-118
17. c	121-122
18. a	126
19. c	126
20. d	124

SEXUALITY AND SEXUAL EXPRESSION THROUGHOUT LIFE

6

CHAPTER OBJECTIVES

Based upon their reading and careful consideration of Chapter Six, students should:

1. be aware of the impact of sexual identity, sexual orientation, and the influence of sexual scripts on one's sexuality.

2. be able to compare and contrast biological theories of sexual orientation with social constructionist theories of sexual orientation.

3. be able to identify the social and psychological factors that contribute to the formation of a gay/lesbian/bisexual identity.

4. be aware of the similarities of modern and traditional sexual scripts.

5. be able to explain how the double standard contributes to the increasing rate of rape and other sexual assaults on women.

6. be able to identify the stages that couples progress through enroute to the first experience of sexual intercourse.

7. recognize the influence that parents, popular culture, peers, and sex education programs have on the development of one's sexual identity.

8. be familiar with the role of sexual fantasy and foreplay that typically precedes sexual intercourse.

9. be able to identify and explain the stages of Masters and Johnson's sexual response cycle.

10.   be able to identify the tasks that adolescents face as they prepare to become involved in a premarital sexual relationship.

11.   be able to identify the reasons adolescents become involved in premarital sexual relationships.

12.   understand the dynamics of marital sex, including the frequency of sex, the relationship between sex and marital happiness and the question of whether the importance of sex is exaggerated.

13.   be able to define extramarital sex in terms of its macro and micro explanations; be familiar with the rates associated with these activities, the signs of possible infidelity, and what happens when affairs end; and understand the consequences of this behavior for family relationships.

14.   be familiar with sexuality and the aging process, including the biological changes in sexual functioning due to aging, the implications of the middle years of life for women and men (menopause, the male climacteric, and the mid-life crisis), sexuality among the elderly, and the double standard of aging.

15.   be aware of the diversity in homosexual relationships and the costs and benefits of homosexual behavior.

16.   be familiar with the major sexually transmitted diseases (STDs), including HIV and AIDS, and the various behaviors, both heterosexual and homosexual, that are related to these health conditions.

CHAPTER OVERVIEW

This chapter focuses on how culture shapes our sexual development, attitudes, and actions. It is noted that sexual behavior changes throughout life and varies over the years. Cross-cultural research shows that there is great latitude in defining what is "normal" or acceptable.

SEXUALITY AND HUMAN DEVELOPMENT

Our sexuality is a product of our sexual identity, sexual orientation, and the influence of sexual scripts. Sexuality is a multidimensional concept that incorporates psychological, biological, and sociological components (e.g. sexual response, sexual desire, and gender roles).

Our sexual identity incorporates a sexual orientation so that people prefer partners of the same sex (homosexuals), the opposite sex (heterosexuals), or of either sex (bisexuals). (Note that many gay men and lesbians deny or try to suppress their sexual preference due to heterosexism in our society.) Two categories of theories on sexual orientation are discussed – biological theories argue that genes, sex hormones, or anatomy determines sexual preference; social constructionist theories hold that sexual orientation is largely the result of social and environmental factors. (At this point in time, many researchers speculate that sexual orientation might be shaped by a combination of genetic and cultural factors.)

While researchers are interested in determining the roots of sexual orientation for scientific reasons, many gays and lesbians have mixed feelings about the research. On one hand, establishing that sexual orientation is genetic would disprove those who say that homosexuality is perverse and who instruct gays to seek counseling for a cure. On the other hand, some lesbians and gay men fear that genetic proof of a person's homosexuality could lead to new forms of discrimination.

Many researchers assert that gender is a more powerful distinguishing factor among people than sexual orientation is – i.e., there are more similarities between heterosexual and homosexual men than between lesbians and gays. Researchers have found that: 1) lesbians and heterosexual women usually have monogamous relationships, while gays and heterosexual men are more likely to have more than one lover at a time; 2) for lesbians and heterosexual women, love-sex usually go hand-in-hand while many gays and heterosexual men often separate intimacy and sex; 3) lesbians and heterosexual women are much less likely to be aroused by visual stimuli than are gays and heterosexual men; 4) both lesbians and heterosexual women are less interested in sex with strangers or in public places than are many gays and heterosexual men, 5) whereas many gays and heterosexual men want as much sexual variety as possible, most women seek long-term partners and less exotic experimentation, and 6) it is heterosexual and homosexual men who are the mainstay of such industries as prostitution, pornography, topless or gay bars, escort services, and adult bookstores.

Sexual scripts specify the norms for legitimate or unacceptable sexual activity, the eligibility of sexual partners, and the boundaries of sexual behavior. Although sexual scripts are less traditional today than they were in the past, the double standard is still widespread. Men and women have different sexual scripts and despite the sexual revolution, modern sexual scripts are not very different from more traditional scripts.

A discussion of why we have sexual relations indicates that once people have committed to a relationship, sexual relations serve a variety of functions. A review of the literature on sex in close relationships concluded that sex can be: an expression of love and affection that is emotional, social (encouraging and sharing friends), intellectual (promoting the sharing of ideas), and recreational. Sex can also encourage self-disclosure, be an important factor in maintaining a relationship, and provide an exchange of resources. Besides these sociological and psychological reasons for sex, biologists maintain that there is an essential evolutionary connection between sexual pleasure and reproduction.

HOW WE LEARN ABOUT SEX

What we see as normal sexual behavior is neither "natural" nor "instinctive" but is learned in a societal context. We become sexual over time. In the normative stage, children learn gender roles and related values and norms about both appropriate and inappropriate sexual expression. Parents (or other caretakers) and popular culture have considerable control over the types and influences to which the child is exposed. In the informational stage in early adolescence, young people learn about sexual anatomy and physiology, primarily from peers, but also from sex education programs in schools. In the behavioral stage in late adolescence and young adulthood, people engage in sexual activity and learn the behavioral aspects of sexuality from a partner.

SEXUAL BEHAVIORS

A discussion of sexual behaviors begins with sexual fantasies. Males and females both fantasize about sex, but due to their different sexual scripts, they fantasize differently. Although the actual content of sexual fantasies differs between males and females, most fantasies have very similar themes. Sexual fantasies are healthy in providing a safety-valve for pent-up feelings, boosting the self-image, and anticipating prospective sexual behavior.

Masturbation (self-pleasuring that involves some form of direct physical stimulation) may or may not result in orgasm. Although we know today that masturbation causes no physical harm, Victorian attitudes still linger. Variables that impact on the frequency of masturbation include gender, marital status, education, and ethnicity. Frequency of masturbation, like that of other sexual activities, declines with age. Masturbation can be as sexually satisfying as intercourse, and it does not hinder the development of social relationships during young adulthood or during marriage. Masturbation fulfills several needs - it relieves sexual tension, provides a safe means of sexual expression, increases sexual self-confidence, and may ultimately transfer valuable learning to two-person lovemaking.

Petting, which includes touching, stroking, mutual masturbation, and fondling various parts of the body (especially the breasts and genitalia), is generally more accepted than intercourse because it is less intimate and doesn't result in pregnancy. Recently, some researchers are including oral sex in definitions of petting. Oral sex (fellatio or cunnilingus) can be performed singly or simultaneously. While many adolescent couples stop at petting, there may also be oral-genital contract either preceding intercourse or instead of it.

An overview of sexual intercourse reveals that average monthly sexual intercourse peaks between ages 25 and 34 and then declines over the years as people develop other interests besides sex that become a high priority in maintaining a family or relationship. Having an easily accessible partner (such as in marriage or cohabitation) seems to have the largest impact on the frequency of sexual activity. Masters and Johnson's sexual response cycle (desire, excitement, orgasm and resolution) is discussed next. Three myths about sexual response conclude this section. They are:

1)   the association by men of a relationship between penis size and orgasm (of which there is no evidence);

2)   the belief that the male can always tell if his partner has had an orgasm; and

3)   the idea that simultaneous orgasm is the ultimate peak in sexual pleasure (although simultaneous orgasm can be exhilarating, so can independent orgasms).

SEXUALITY THROUGHOUT LIFE

The first sexual experience can be happy and satisfying; it can also be a source of worry, disappointment, or guilt. Premarital sex has become more socially acceptable for adults over the years, but a large percentage of these adult men and women believe that premarital intercourse for teenagers aged 14 to 16 is almost always wrong. Despite this disapproval, many adolescents are having premarital sex. There are numerous reasons for the increase in premarital sex among adolescents, including earlier maturation, peer pressure, environmental factors, cultural attitudes and expectations, and nonvoluntary factors. Adolescents are often reluctant to discuss sex with their parents.

Like their younger counterparts, more college-aged students are engaging in sex; premarital intercourse has increased considerably since the mid-1960s, especially among women—the gap between men and women has decreased substantially in the past three decades. College-aged males and females often engage in sex for different reasons. The double standard is alive and well. Virginity and sexual abstinence are not cultural dinosaurs and, in fact, several factors encourage both of these behaviors.

Marital sex has received far less attention in the research literature than has premarital or extramarital sex. Historically, research shows that married women were interested in and concerned about sex long before it was fashionable to talk about it in public. Available research shows that marital sexual activity typically decreases with the age and longevity of married couples. Despite this, married couples report that sex can be satisfying in the absence of actual sexual intercourse. Married couples who report a decline in sex attribute the change to such things as work, child rearing, fatigue, and familiarity. Most observers conclude that the general quality of a marital relationship is more important than the sex. Some think that the importance of sex has been exaggerated.

Many stereotypes exist about sexuality and aging. While there are physiological changes regarding sexuality in both females and males as aging takes place, many of these have been exaggerated. For both sexes, the physiological changes that come with aging by no means preclude sexual activity or lessen its pleasure. The media has contributed to the exaggerated view of sex as extremely important in later life. In the middle years women undergo menopause and men may experience a so-called climacteric, but the latter change may be more psychological than physiological. It has only been in recent years that menopause has been studied seriously; whether there really is a male climacteric is controversial. It may be that the male "change of life" is a more general "mid-life crisis." The middle years can produce "burnout" for both sexes, and this can reduce sexual passion. Historically, the elderly have been seen as "sexless." Although sexual activity declines with advancing age, many elderly people still enjoy sex. As people age, the biggest impediment to sex is usually not lack of desire or ability but a lack of available sex partners; this is especially true for women. It's not until about the age of 70 that the frequency of sexual activity in both men and women begins to decline significantly, and this is generally due to health problems. The double standard persists throughout old age: Men in their sixties are considered "distinguished," while their female counterparts are regarded as just "old."

Extramarital affairs usually do not last more than 1 or 2 years, and only 10 percent result in marriage. The effects of such affairs can have devastating consequences for family relationships. There are at least five *macro* reasons for extramarital sex: economic recessions and depressions, the changing purpose of marriage, the anonymity of urban life, the longer length of marriages, and the effects of various social movements. The primary *micro* reasons are: attitudes about sex are changing, social roles are changing, the need for emotional satisfaction or the need to escape emotional isolation, a rise in expectations about the quality of life and a temptation to try different sexual experiences, a means of revenge or retaliation toward a spouse, to provide a way out of marriage, and greater opportunities for extramarital sex today. Top psychologists suggest that there are usually signs that an extramarital affair is going on. Affairs end in different ways, including shock-out, drag-out, and wind-down. Most extramarital affairs devastate the entire family. Extramarital sex has broad structural implications for society as a whole.

Homosexuals share many of the same sexual characteristics, problems, and activities in expressing love, engaging in sexual activities, and raising children as do heterosexuals. There is substantial diversity in homosexual relationships. Bell and Weinberg found five primary types of such relationships: close-coupled, open-coupled, functional, dysfunctional, and asexual. Sexual behavior among homosexuals is, in many ways, similar to that of heterosexuals. Most of the differences between homosexual and heterosexual relationships are legal. Homosexual relationships are fragile for four major reasons: the lack of kinship solidarity due to secrecy, the fear of dissolution, increased role stress due to ambiguous expectations and duties, and problems associated with becoming parents. There are also some advantages: egalitarianism, less role bound relationships, greater knowledge about emotional and physical needs, and longer-term relationships among lesbians due to women not having been socialized to seek sexual conquests.

SEXUALLY TRANSMITTED DISEASES, HIV, AND AIDS

Sexually transmitted diseases (STDs) are infections that are spread by contact, sexual or nonsexual, with body parts or fluids that harbor specific microorganisms (generally bacterial or viral). One of the most serious (and still fatal) STDs is the human immunodeficiency virus (HIV) that causes acquired immunodeficiency syndrome, or AIDS. Although first discovered among gay men, AIDS is now spreading fastest among heterosexuals. Heterosexuals with the highest risk for HIV infection are teenagers, adults with multiple sex partners, people who suffer from other STDs and people who live in areas where AIDS is prevalent.

Although AIDS cannot be cured, it can be prevented. AIDS is disproportionately high among people of color. Cultural factors in the incidence of AIDS are many and varied. Although AIDS among heterosexuals is spreading faster than among homosexuals, many gay men continue to have unprotected intercourse. AIDS does not appear to be a deterrent to premarital intercourse; although the virus has encouraged the use of condoms, many teenagers and young adults are still engaging in high-risk sexual behavior, such as having intercourse with multiple partners without the protection of a condom.

CURRENT APPLICATIONS

1. On page 143 of your text, Figure 6.2 presents some data drawn from a 1994 nationwide survey of sexual behavior; it is pointed out that these data surprised some observers. Are you surprised by the results of this survey? Based upon your own personal knowledge, do you think this data is accurate? Assuming the validity and reliability of this investigation, using your "sociological eye," think about why there appears to be a gap between what people *expected* to find and what the researchers *actually* determined. What do you think explains this divergence?

2. Form a discussion group within your class in order to discuss the content of any sex education program that operated within the public school system you attended. Perhaps one of the members of this group will have attended a school where there was no formal program in place. Ask this person to vocalize how the absence of such a program affected his/her own attitudes toward sexuality. On the other hand, perhaps one of the discussion group participants will have attended a school that had a very progressive sex education program. Compare his/her views with those of the person who had no (or less) formal sex education in school.

3. Consider how the myths and misinformation surrounding the spread of AIDS have affected Americans' attitudes toward homosexuality and non-marital sex. How do you feel about a national survey of sexual attitudes and values? Do you think one should be conducted? Why or why not? Do you find it disturbing that no such study has been conducted or is forthcoming? Given the gravity of the AIDS epidemic, why would a society like ours be reluctant to want to find out everything possible about people's sexual behavior?

4. If your sexual orientation is heterosexual, consider the differences between your attitudes and values about sex in comparison to your

significant other, lover, or intimate companion. If you are homosexual or bisexual, consider how your personal attitudes may have varied with men or women with whom you have had a sexual relationship. Consider these differences in light of the text's discussion of gender variations in attitudes toward sexuality.

5.   Since the appearance of Acquired Immune Deficiency Syndrome (AIDS) in the early 1980s, the incidence of the virus has *declined* significantly among homosexuals in our society. On the other hand, AIDS has become more common place among heterosexuals. Admittedly, this is partially explained by intravenous transmission in conjunction with illegal drug use, but there is not doubt that the AIDS virus is a threat to heterosexuals who are engaging in unprotected sexual intercourse. As pointed out in the text, it is interesting that there persists a great deal of premarital and nonmarital sexual interaction despite the threat of AIDS. How seriously do you think heterosexuals are taking AIDS into account in their premarital and nonmarital sex lives? You may wish to pose a version of this question to some of your friends, recording their responses for reference later on. Then, compile their answers and consider the implications.

6.   As your author points out in Chapter Six, Americans seem to be almost obsessed with sex—we worry about our sexual prowess, we are apprehensive about the size, shape, and overall performance of the sexually related organs of our bodies; we are apprehensive about the frequency with which we have sex, and we are anxious about sex as we age. Why do you think that there are so many "hang-ups" about sex in our society? Is it our Victorian heritage? Is it the nature of Judeo-Christian religions? And what about the current conservative movement in the United States? What effects do you think that this movement will have on future attitudes toward human sexuality?

7.   When thinking about co-marital relationships, we usually think of heterosexual involvements. Put yourself in the following situation: You are married to a spouse of ten years and have three children – a son ten years of age, another son who is eight years of age, and a daughter who is three. Your spouse informs you that he/she met a same-sex person who they feel an emotional and physical attraction to and need to find out just where he/she stands in terms of their sexual identity (as they approach their fortieth birthday). Your spouse asks that you "be there" for them and they will keep you apprised of their feelings. They ask that you keep this information confidential, and while they can promise nothing,

they will be completely honest with you. Answer the following questions:

   a. Since the third party is the same sex as your spouse, do you feel less threatened than if they were of the opposite sex?

   b. Does their "being up front" about their attraction to this other person make this a more tolerable situation than if it were a clandestine relationship?

   c. How would you react to your spouse's request for you to "be strong" and let them "work this out" in their own mind?

   d. Assuming this is part of a mid-life crisis, how long a time period is reasonable for your spouse to determine if they are heterosexual, bisexual, or homosexual/lesbian?

   e. What would your response be should your spouse end their same-sex emotional and physical involvement and offer to come back to the children and you?

   f. Should they choose to continue their same-sex co-marital involvement and seek a divorce, would their sexual identity be a factor in determining who would raise the children? Why or why not?

KEY TERMS FILL-IN

1.   Our sexual _____ is our awareness of ourselves as male or female and how we express our sexual values, attitudes, feelings, and beliefs, and is part of how we define who we are and what roles we play.

2.   Sexual _____ refers to the sexual drives that we learn through sexual experiences and feelings of enjoyment or dissatisfaction during sexual activity.

3.   Sexual _____ encompasses the biological aspects of sexuality that include experiencing pleasure or orgasm.

4.   Behavior that women and men enact according to culturally prescribed expectations comprises our _____ roles.

5.   A _____ is a person who is sexually attracted to people of the same sex; in contrast, a _____ is attracted to partners of the opposite sex.

6.   _____ are sexually attracted to members of both sexes.

7.   _____ is a belief that heterosexuality is superior and more "natural" than homosexuality.

8.   _____ theories of sexual orientation argue that genes, sex hormones, or anatomy determine sexual behavior.

9.   _____ _____ theories hold that sexual orientation is largely the result of social and environmental factors.

10. A _____ specifies the formal or informal norms for legitimate or unacceptable sexual activity.

11. According to Brooks (1995), the "_____ Syndrome" represents one of the most malignant forces in contemporary relationships because it objectifies women.

12. The word _____ specifically refers to vaginal-penile intercourse.

13. _____ is the cessation of the menstrual cycle and the loss of reproductive capacity.

14. The hypothetical change of life experienced by men which is analogous to female menopause is called a _____ _____.

15. The fear and hatred of homosexuality is called _____.

16. Two of the oldest known sexually transmitted diseases are _____ and _____.

17. _____ is a degenerative condition that attacks the body's immune system and renders it unable to fight a number of diseases.

MULTIPLE CHOICE

1.   Our sexuality is the product of our:
     a.   sexual identity.
     b.   sexual desire.
     c.   sexual response.
     d.   all of the above.

2. Research on the cause(s) of homosexuality have established that:
    a. environment determines sexual orientation.
    b. there is a "gay gene" that determines one's sexual orientation.
    c. sexual orientation is probably shaped by a combination of genetic and cultural factors.
    d. gay men with twin brothers and lesbian women with twin sisters have consistently reported that their identical twin is also gay.

3. According to the text's discussion of sexual orientation and gender:
    a. lesbians and heterosexual women usually have monogamous relationships.
    b. many gay and heterosexual men often separate emotional intimacy and sex.
    c. heterosexual and homosexual men are the mainstays of such industries as prostitution, pornography, topless or gay bars, escort services, and adult bookstores.
    d. all of the above

4. The formal and informal norms for legitimate or unacceptable sexual activity, the eligibility of sexual partners, and the boundaries of sexual behavior in terms of time and place, are specified by:
    a. sexual scripts.
    b. sexual revolutions.
    c. authority figures.
    d. commodity markets.

5. According to Brooks, the "_____ syndrome" represents one of the most malignant forces in contemporary relationships between men and women because it objectifies women.
    a. second shift
    b. double standard
    c. pink collar
    d. centerfold

6. A review of the literature on sex in close relationships indicates that sex:
    a. can increase intimacy and a feeling of closeness.
    b. can encourage self-disclosure.
    c. fosters interdependence because the partners depend on each other for sexual satisfaction.
    d. all of the above are true about sex in a close relationship.

7.   What we see as normal sexual behavior is:
     a.   "natural" sexual behavior.
     b.   "instinctive" sexual behavior.
     c.   learned in a societal context.
     d.   all of the above are true to normal sexual behavior.

8.   Regarding the effect of parents on how children think and feel
     about sexuality:
     a.   ideally, parents should be the first and best sex educators
          because they are experienced and have the children's best
          interests at heart.
     b.   many parents underestimate the role they play in their
          children's sex education.
     c.   parents are generally very comfortable talking about sex with
          their children.
     d.   adolescents tend to be eager to discuss sex with their
          parents.

9.   For high school and college students, the most common source of
     knowledge about sex is:
     a.   parents.
     b.   peers.
     c.   sex education courses.
     d.   popular culture.

10. Ward examined the content of the 12 most popular prime-time
     television programs during the mid-1990s starring children aged 2
     to 11 and adolescents aged 12 to 17 and found that:
     a.   sexual content was present in more than one of every four
          interactions.
     b.   frank discussion of sex on television may be healthy but that
          the content of these discussions is still traditional and sex-
          stereotypical.
     c.   many television shows suggest that the purpose of sex is
          almost exclusively recreational rather than procreative.
     d.   all of the above

11. About _____ percent of U.S. adults approve of schools
     providing sex education.
     a.   32
     b.   45
     c.   60
     d.   90

12. In a recent examination of a composite week of 1,351 television shows aired between October 1997 and March 1998, it was determined that _____ of all network prime-time shows contained sexual content and averaged more than five sex scenes per hour.
   a. 37
   b. 47
   c. 57
   d. 67

13. Kirby and Associates (1994) found that the most effective sex education curricula:
   a. focused more on parents as socializing agents than peers.
   b. were more general in their focus rather than emphasizing particular issues.
   c. focused instruction about postponing sexual intercourse on middle school students while information about how to use condoms was aimed at older students.
   d. emphasized the use of professional rather than peer counselors.

14. Research on sexual fantasies indicates that:
   a. most scientists believe that such fantasies are prominent among emotionally unstable individuals.
   b. in some cases, fantasies are mental rehearsals for future sexual experiences.
   c. women who fantasize about "unusual" sex practices are more likely to act them out than men are.
   d. fantasies tend to reduce one's self-image by focusing on one's body-parts rather than the function of sex as a source of intimacy.

15. _____ refers to sexual self-pleasuring that involves some form of direct physical stimulation.
   a. Fornication
   b. Masturbation
   c. Prevarication
   d. Prognostication

16. Research on masturbation indicates that:
   a. many teenagers discover masturbation accidentally.
   b. frequency of masturbation declines with age.
   c. there are large differences in frequency of masturbation racially and ethnically.
   d. all of the above are true.

17.   _____ includes touching, stroking, mutual masturbation, and fondling various parts of the body, especially the breasts and genitalia.
    a.   Fornication
    b.   Prevarication
    c.   Prognostication
    d.   Petting

18.   Which of the following is NOT one of the four stages in Master's and Johnson's sexual response cycle?
    a.   sexual stirring
    b.   desire
    c.   excitement
    d.   resolution

19.   Which of the following is a common myth about sexual response?
    a.   Association between clitoris, breast, or penis size and orgasm
    b.   A male can always tell if his partner has had an orgasm
    c.   Simultaneous orgasm is the ultimate peak in sexual pleasure
    d.   All of the above are common myths about sexual pleasuring

20.   The text offers which of the following as reasons for premarital sex?
    a.   peer pressure
    b.   parental and environmental factors
    c.   cultural attitudes and expectations
    d.   all of the above

21.   _____ sexual activity typically decreases with age and the longevity of the marriage.
    a.   Premarital
    b.   Extramarital
    c.   Marital
    d.   Intermarital

22.   Whether there is a(n) _____, or change of life analogous to female menopause, is not known for sure.
    a.   impotency period
    b.   Viagra-necessity
    c.   male menopause
    d.   male climacteric

23. _____ usually begins in a woman's mid-forties to early fifties.
    a.   Mid-life crisis
    b.   Menopause
    c.   Climacteric
    d.   Impotence

24. The text observes that whereas gray-haired men in their 60s are considered "distinguished," their female counterparts are just "old." This is an example of what is referred to as:
    a.   Murphy's law of aging.
    b.   the gender gap in aging.
    c.   the double standard of aging.
    d.   Peter's aging principle.

25. People use the terms "affair," "infidelity," "adultery," and "_____," interchangeably.
    a.   premarital
    b.   intermarital
    c.   extramarital
    d.   promiscuous

26. Which of the following is NOT one of the *macro* explanations cited in the text for extramarital sex?
    a.   changing social roles.
    b.   economic recessions and depressions
    c.   the anonymity of urban life
    d.   the purpose of marriage has changed for many people

27. Which of the following is NOT one of the *micro* explanations cited in the text for extramarital sex?
    a.   changing attitudes about sex in general
    b.   a need for emotional satisfaction or a need to escape emotional isolation
    c.   the desire for revenge or retaliation
    d.   individual alienation

28. Many social scientists consider _____ a deeply rooted insecurity.
    a.   homophobia
    b.   heterosexuality
    c.   bisexuality
    d.   masturbation

29. According to the text's discussion of AIDS:
    a. the incidence of AIDS is very low among people of color.
    b. AIDS can usually be cured.
    c. cultural factors in the incidence of AIDS are many and varied.
    d. AIDS is spreading faster among homosexuals than among heterosexuals.

30. The reason(s) why Latinos are believed to have high HIV and AIDS rates, especially from heterosexual contact, is/are because:
    a. both adolescents and adults know less and have more misconceptions about HIV transmission than do non-Hispanic whites.
    b. many Latinos still believe the myth that one can discern an HIV person by the way he or she looks.
    c. they are less likely than non-Hispanic women to use condoms during intercourse.
    d. All of the above are reasons for the HIV and AIDS rates among Latinos.

ANSWERS

KEY TERMS FILL-IN

ANSWERS	PAGE NUMBERS
1. identity	131
2. desire	131
3. response	131
4. gender	131
5. homosexual (gay); heterosexual (straight)	131
6. Bisexuals (bi's)	132
7. Heterosexism	132
8. Biological	132
9. Social constructionist	133
10. sexual scripts	134
11. Centerfold	135
12. coitus	145
13. Menopause	153
14. male climactic	153
15. homohobia	158
16. syphillis and gonorrhea	159
17. AIDS (acquired immunodeficiency syndrome)	160

MULTIPLE CHOICE

ANSWERS		PAGE NUMBERS
1.	d	131
2.	c	132-133
3.	d	134
4.	a	134
5.	d	135
6.	d	136
7.	c	138
8.	a	138; 140-141
9.	b	141
10.	d	141
11.	d	142
12.	d	141
13.	d	142
14.	b	142-143
15.	b	143
16.	a	144
17.	d	144
18.	a	146-147
19.	d	148
20.	d	149-150
21.	c	152
22.	d	153
23.	b	153
24.	c	155
25.	c	155
26.	a	156
27.	d	156
28.	a	158
29.	c	160-162
30.	d	161

7

CHOOSING OTHERS: DATING AND MATE SELECTION

CHAPTER OBJECTIVES

Based upon their reading and careful consideration of Chapter Seven, students should:

1. be familiar with the reasons for and the manifest and latent functions of dating.

2. be able to identify and discuss the various traditional and contemporary forms of dating, including traditional-contemporary combinations.

3. be familiar with the two general categories of contemporary dating—casual and serious—and be able to identify the forms of dating discussed in the text: hanging out, getting together, "goin' with," serious casual dating, serious dating, and traditional-contemporary combinations, including: cruising, proms, and homecoming parties, mixers, and dinner dates.

4. be familiar with the contemporary mate-selection methods discussed in the text: personal classified advertisements, mail-order brides, marriage bureaus, and computer cupids (including electronic networks), and be able to discuss the advantages and disadvantages of each method.

5. be familiar with the choices and constraints in dating and mate selection; understand the permanent-availability model; and be able to define endogamy and exogamy and understand how our dating and mate selection behavior is shaped by endogamous and exogamous rules, including ethnicity, race, religion, age, and social class.

6. be familiar with the three mate-selection theories discussed in the text: filter theory, exchange theory, and equity theory.

7.   be able to discuss the six "filters" for endogamy (propinquity, social networks, values, sexual orientation, length of courtship, and physical attractiveness); and understand how HIV/AIDS has narrowed the pool of eligible dating partners.

8.   understand social-exchange theory and equity theory as explanations for our mate-selection choices.

9.   be familiar with the cross-cultural currents in mate selection in the United States and other Western nations.

10.   be able to discuss the problems in dating and mate selection, including the implications of power, control, and aggression; courtship violence; and acquaintance/date rape.

11.   be familiar with the reasons for courtship violence and date rape (misogyny, gender-role expectations and media images, and peer pressure); understand the consequences of these behaviors, and the risk factors involved (use of alcohol and other drugs and dating location/activity); and be able to offer some possible solutions.

12.   be able to compare and contrast the different ways in which men and women deal with breaking up and be familiar with the use of dating contracts and detective agencies.

CHAPTER OVERVIEW

The courtship process is romanticized in the media, but it is rarely this predictable; there are both exhilarating and excruciating elements to courtship. The mate selection process may be more open than in the past, but there remains a variety of important variables which shape our mate-selection behavior.

WHY DO WE DATE? (Manifest-Latent Functions of Dating)

Dating serves both manifest and latent functions. Among the manifest functions are recreation, companionship, and a step in mate selection; among the latent functions are socialization, gaining social status, fulfilling ego needs, and opportunities for sexual experimentation and intimacy. Manifest and latent functions usually overlap and change over time.

THE DATING SPECTRUM

Dating is changing, for both adolescents and adults. Traditional dating dominated through the 1970s, at least among the middle classes, and is a fairly formal model of meeting potential spouses. Although less common today, traditional dating still exists. The process has changed, however, as many adolescents and young adults have forsaken traditional dating (and formal coming-out parties or the *quinceanera* among Latinos) for more informal strategies such as hanging out, getting together, and going together ("goin' with"). The modern "going together" is a compromise between going steady and getting together. Also note that many undergraduates socialize in unpartnered groups or "pack dating." Pack dating is popular because it provides recreation without feeling pressured to make a commitment or getting romantically involved. It also appeals to students holding down jobs while carrying high course loads, many who may feel they don't have the time and energy to find dates or maintain one-on-one relationships. In addition, if some of the participants become sexually active, pack dating may be an attempt to deal with the risk of disease.

Perhaps the least gender-typed dating, at least on first dates, is between same-sex partners. Researchers have found little gender typing compared to heterosexual dating. Both partners participated more equally in orchestrating the date, maintaining the conversation, and initiating physical contact.

Several dating patterns incorporate both traditional customs and contemporary innovations, including cruising, proms and homecoming parties, mixers, and dinner dates.

MEETING OTHERS

Adults employ a variety of mate-selection methods to meet potential spouses, including personal classified ads, mail-order brides, marriage bureaus, and computer-dating services. A recent variation on personal classified ads is "voice personals," utilizing the telephone. Mail-order services publish photographs and descriptions of available women, but this system has been abusive of those involved. In some countries, classified ads and especially marriage bureaus have replaced the old-fashioned, community-based matchmaker. Many computer-dating services ("computer cupids") use videotapes in order to acquaint clients with each other. The most recent computer cupids are electronic networks, some have even had weddings online, these arrangements can also become offensive or intimidating.

There are both choices and constraints in Americans' dating and mate-selection activities. Although there are more choices in the methods used, much mate-selection behavior is shaped by exogamous and endogamous rules that define appropriate mates in terms of race, ethnicity, religion, age, and social class. Hypergamy (marriage with someone who is from a higher socioeconomic background) is more characteristic of women than men.

Sociologists have suggested several theoretical perspectives to explain mate selection. Three that are used most often are filter theory, exchange theory, and equity theory. From the perspective of filter theory, dating may be seen as a sifting process. This field is further narrowed by geography (propinquity), age and social networks, values, sexual orientation, length of courtship, and physical attractiveness. Most recently, the presence of HIV infections and AIDS has been added to the selection process. Propinquity plays a major role in mate selection; although families are more geographically mobile today, interacting with people we see on a regular basis is still an important factor in dating and mating. The vast majority of singles meet their dating partners through such social networks as mutual friends. Values have not changed that much with regard to desirable traits in a future mate. One rule of exogamy is that we must marry someone of the opposite sex, but some societies extend legal recognition to same-sex marriages; in the United States, there is increasing recognition of "domestic partners." There is a strong correlation between the length of time spent dating and marital satisfaction. Physical attractiveness has been determined to be more important for men than it is for women in choosing a date.

According to social exchange theory, prospective partners are attracted to those who will provide them with the best possible "deal" in a relationship; people will begin and remain in a relationship if the rewards are high and the costs are low.

Equity theory is designed to predict when individuals will perceive that they are justly treated and how they will react when they find themselves enmeshed in unjust relationships. People who find themselves in an inequitable relationship will try to restore equity.

A GLOBAL VIEW: DESIRABLE MATE CHARACTERISTICS AND SELECTION

There are a number of important cross-cultural variations in mate selection. Unlike the United States and some other Western nations, most countries around the world do not have "open" courtship systems. In these traditional societies, the dowry is still an important basis for mate selection; parents will arrange marriages for their children; and these unions are generally restricted to members of the same culture; they also prohibit marriage between people of different religions or races. Freedom of choice in mate selection largely depends on a country's rate of industrialization and the economic status of women. Some countries in Asia are experiencing dramatic changes in the way people meet and select mates. For example, in China, finding a mate has become a community affair in which both public and private sectors participate.

HARMFUL DATING RELATIONSHIPS: POWER, CONTROL, AND SEXUAL AGGRESSION

In the United States and other countries around the world, dating can be fun and may fulfill important functions for mate selection, but it can also be disappointing and stressful. Courtship can represent crisis and there are many risks and problems. Power, control, and aggression are key words here, and sociologist Willard Waller's *principle of least interest* is useful in explaining the balance of power in the traditional male-female dating and courtship relationship. Courtship violence is widespread and although both women and men can be victims, women usually resort to violence in self-defense and they also sustain more physical injuries than men. Courtship violence is rarely a one-time event. Women are often victimized through sexual pressure, violence, acquaintance or date rape, and other forms of aggression. Most sexual aggression and date rapes occur in normal situations that seem safe and familiar; because women are still "blamed" for becoming involved in these situations, the first step is to recognize and avoid some of the risks: unfamiliar partners, power differentials, alcohol and drug use, dating activities and locations, and particular attitudes. There are many different reasons for courtship violence and date rape, including misogyny, gender-role expectations, media messages, and peer pressure. There are many damaging consequences of courtship violence and date rape. Most of these incidents occur in situations that seem safe and familiar. Two of the greatest factors for sexual aggression include the use of alcohol or other drugs and high-risk activities and locations. Because violent behavior and rape are learned, they can be unlearned. Solutions are needed on three levels: individual, organizational, and societal.

BREAKING UP

Nearly half of all dating relationships break up before marriage. The reasons for breakups include unequal commitment on the part of each partner, arguments, pressure from parents, geographic separation, deception, avoidance of open communication, and boredom. There are important differences between men and women when it comes to breaking up: women tend to see more problems in the relationship than men do.

There are more choices in mate selection today than ever before, but there are also many constraints.

CURRENT APPLICATIONS

1. Seek out a member of the "Baby Boom" generation (people who were born between 1945 and the mid 1960s). Ask this person to comment on what "dating" was like during his or her high school and college years. Ask about the double standard in dating behavior (i.e. the tradition of "boy asking girl for a date," but not vice versa); about "going steady," and, if the person was in college during the late 1960s and early 70s, ask him or her to comment on the doctrine of *in loco parentis* (the school being responsible for the student while he or she is at college). There were no co-educational dormitories. Again, the double standard applied: College women were subjected to many curfews that men were not required to adhere to. After you have completed your conversation with this man or woman, consider his/her comments in light of Benokraitis' discussion of modern versus "traditional" dating.

2. How large do you think your individual "field of eligibles" is? If you are already married, consider what demographic ingredients affected your choice: age, race, religion, socioeconomic status (income, education, occupation, geographic location, your parents' opinions, etc.) If you are planning on eventually marrying, do you think that the person in question will be "like" yourself or different? After you have thought about these issues, integrate your thinking with the text's discussion of endogamy.

3. Is there any conspicuous "rating and dating" on your college or university campus? Can you think of some examples? Do they involve socioeconomic status? How? What about prestige? For example, if there are fraternities and sororities at your school, are there any patterns of dating present—i.e. are some sorority women more likely to date certain fraternity men?

4. Is date rape a *new* phenomenon? Or, is it that up until recently, women "gave in" to pressures placed upon them by their dates to have sex? There are many familiar phrases from the past that help to shed light on this issue: "If you love me, you'll do it." "Come on, I just spent $100 on drinks and dinner..." "But, will you still respect me in the morning?" Talk to some of your friends about

80

what it means when a woman says "No" to a sexual advance. Some men and women who are older may give different answers than those who are younger. Consider these responses in terms of how the phenomenon of date rape appears to be contemporary.

KEY TERMS FILL-IN

1. _____ is the process of meeting people socially for possible mate selection.

2. Some sociologists describe the courtship process as a _____ _____ .

3. A contemporary form of dating where undergraduates socialize without feeling pressured to make a commitment or get romantically involved is called _____ dating.

4. _____ _____ suggests that people searching for partners tend to go through a process of filtering out eligible people according to certain specific criteria and thus narrow the pool of potential partners.

5. Geographical closeness or _____, plays a major role in mate selection.

6. _____ is marriage with someone who is from a higher socioeconomic background and is more characteristic of women than men.

7. _____ theory tries to predict when individuals will perceive injustice and how they will react when they find themselves enmeshed in inequitable relations.

8. In some Mediterranean and East-Asian societies, _____ are important foundations for mate selection.

9. _____ _____ can start at a very early age.

10. _____ _____ refers to unwanted, forced sexual intercourse in the context of a dating situation.

11. _____ _____ refers to rape of a person who knows or is familiar with the rapist.

MULTIPLE CHOICE

1. According to the text, dating is a:
   a. highly standardized way of meeting people.
   b. simple process based on a cost-benefits analysis.
   c. declining in popularity due to the AIDS crisis.
   d. considerably more complicated than just going out and having fun.

2. The process in which prospective spouses compare the assets and liabilities of eligible partners is known as:
   a. exogamy.
   b. misogyny.
   c. courtship.
   d. marriage market.

3. Which of the following is NOT a manifest function of dating cited in the text?
   a. recreation
   b. companionship
   c. socialization
   d. a step in mate selection

4. Which of the following is NOT a latent function of dating cited in the text?
   a. companionship
   b. gaining social status
   c. fulfilling ego needs
   d. opportunities for sexual experimentation and intimacy

5. Which of the following is NOT a *contemporary* form of dating?
   a. hanging out
   b. going steady
   c. getting together
   d. "goin' with"

6. According to the text, the *quinceanera*:
   a. may be translated loosely as "five years."
   b. is a Latino form of "going steady."
   c. is a coming-out party in some Latino communities that celebrates a girl's entrance into adulthood.
   d. is the female equivalent of the *machismo* ritual for boys.

7. When a person recognizes that a woman or man might actually fit their romantic vision of a relationship and decides that he or she wants to get closer, this step is referred to as:
   a. "goin' with."
   b. getting together.
   c. hanging out.
   d. serious dating.

8. Which of the following is NOT one of the dating patterns representing a combination of traditional and contemporary innovations?
   a. serious dating
   b. homecoming parties
   c. proms
   d. dinner dates

9. Which of the following is NOT one of the contemporary mate-selection methods discussed in the text?
   a. personal classified advertisements
   b. mail-order brides
   c. marriage bureaus
   d. All of the above are contemporary mate-selection processes cited in the text.

10. The text suggests that the least gender-typed dating, particularly on first dates, is between:
    a. dinner dates.
    b. "getting together."
    c. same-sex partners.
    d. African American men and women.

11. Often women will exchange their youth or beauty for a man's higher education, income, or social status. This is known as:
    a. homogamy.
    b. hypergamy.
    c. exogamy.
    d. heterogamy.

12. It is highly unlikely that children living in upper-class neighborhoods will even meet those in middle-class, much less working class families. This is due to:
    a. snobbishness.
    b. aloofness.
    c. propinquity.
    d. discrimination.

13. Pack dating has become popular among undergraduate students because:
    a. it is one of the best ways available to find a permanent mate.
    b. group sex is an ever-present possibility.
    c. it doesn't require as much time and energy to find dates or find one-on-one relationships.
    d. all of the above are reasons.

14. The term used by sociologists for males who seek to improve their social standing by marrying up is:
    a. hypogamy.
    b. homogamy.
    c. heterogamy.
    d. There has not been a term coined for males who marry up.

15. In some societies, such as India, _____ rules may prohibit marriage between individuals of similarly named clans.
    a. homogamy
    b. misogyny
    c. exogamy
    d. endogamy

16. In Buss and Barnes' (1986) survey of married couples to determine the most important qualities in a mate, the top-related quality was:
    a. good company.
    b. physically attractive.
    c. an exciting personality.
    d. kindness.

17. In Fein and Schneider's book, *The Rules*, the authors encourage women to:
    a. be honest and open in their relationships with men.
    b. scheme and manipulate men to get marriage proposals.
    c. not call men and rarely return his calls.
    d. establish rules and regulations in a relationship through "good-faith" negotiation.

18. Many researchers find that violence is not a one-time event. Only about _____ percent of the relationships end after the first violent act.
    a. 20
    b. 25
    c. 50
    d. 63

19. Since the mid-1990s, a growing number of college women have reported being raped after their drink was spiked with a sedative known as _____, the date-rape drug.
    a. Rohypnol
    b. Quince
    c. Regimun
    d. Pheusanoyl

20. A major reason cited in the text why people are violent and why many partners stay in abusive relations is
    a. traditional values.
    b. peer pressure.
    c. drug dependency.
    d. masochistic personalities.

21. The victim's loss of ability to trust, guilt, and anger and depression are all effects of:
    a. misogyny.
    b. sexual dysfunction.
    c. date rape.
    d. emotional retardation.

22. People who had dated their former partner for a long time or who feel that they have few desirable alternatives experience:
    a. a new relationship within a short period of time after the breakup.
    b. the greatest distress after a breakup.
    c. a tendency to quickly recover from the breakup.
    d. no desire for a new relationship.

ANSWERS

KEY TERMS FILL-IN

ANSWERS		PAGE NUMBERS
1.	Dating	165
2.	marriage market	165
3.	pack	169
4.	Filter theory	173
5.	propinquity	173
6.	Hypergamy	178
7.	Equity	181

MULTIPLE CHOICE

ANSWERS		PAGE NUMBERS
1.	d	165
2.	d	165
3.	c	166
4.	a	166-167
5.	b	168
6.	c	167
7.	d	168
8.	a	169
9.	d	170-172
10.	c	170
11.	b	178
12.	c	173-174
13.	c	169
14.	d	178
15.	c	179
16.	a	178 (Table 7.1)
17.	b	185
18.	c	186
19.	a	188
20.	b	189
21.	c	189-190 (Table 7.3)
22.	b	190

SINGLEHOOD, COHABITATION, AND OTHER NONMARITAL LIVING ARRANGEMENTS

CHAPTER OBJECTIVES

Based upon their reading and careful consideration of Chapter Eight, students should:

1.   be familiar with the demographics of singlehood.

2.   be able to discuss the reasons why people are remaining single longer, including those circumstances that are unique to Latinos and African Americans.

3.   be familiar with the popular myths about being single and be able to compare these misconceptions with the realities about singlehood.

4.   be able to identify the problems faced by singles in terms of physical and emotional health, age and gender, and housing.

5.   understand the advantages and disadvantages of cohabitation, including the possibility of economic exploitation of women.

6.   be able to discuss cohabitation and the effect (or lack of effect) that it has on marriage.

7.   understand the legal implications of cohabitation.

8.   be able to compare the attitudes toward cohabitative relationships in the United States with similar attitudes in countries like Sweden and Denmark.

9.   be able to compare the characteristics of homosexual couples with those of heterosexual couples, and homosexual families with heterosexual families.

10.	understand the benefits and problems that are unique to homosexual families, particularly with regard to economics and legality.

11.	be familiar with the characteristics of contemporary communal households, including their internal structure and familial relationships.

12.	understand the appeal of communes to senior citizens today.

CHAPTER OVERVIEW

Diverse lifestyles have always existed, but since the 1970s, nontraditional family forms have increased. Although marriage is still the norm, it is an optional lifestyle for larger numbers of people, and many Americans maintain nonmarital households. Chapter Eight examines four of these nontraditional lifestyles: singlehood, cohabitation, homosexual households, and communes.

Household size has been shrinking since the 1940s. A major reason for this decrease is the growing number of people living alone. This does *not* mean that fewer people will get married; on the contrary, since the 1970s, marriage rates have increased. The principal explanation for the increase in singlehood is that people are delaying marriage. The greater acceptance of cohabitation, children born out of wedlock, and divorce has played a role in postponing marriage.

Singles constitute an extremely diverse group; some have been widowed; others have divorced or separated; while still others have never been married. Some singles voluntarily choose their status, while others occupy the status involuntarily; within these two groups, there are "temporary" and "stable" categories.

There are many reasons why the numbers of singles have increased since the 1970s. In the first place, singlehood is no longer seen as a deviant status. In addition, there are both "pushes" and "pulls" toward postponing marriage and remaining single longer. Some of the reasons are demographic, such as the *marriage squeeze*, whereas others reflect more personal choices. Decisions about marriage are often shaped by macro-level phenomena like war, technology, and social movements. Economic factors also play an important role in delaying or encouraging marriage; economic depressions and unemployment tend to postpone marriage for men. The effects of employment on women's tendency to marry are somewhat contradictory. On one hand, being employed increases a woman's chances of meeting eligible men and may enhance her attractiveness as a contributor to a household's financial resources. On the other hand, greater economic independence decreases a woman's interest in early marriage. Employed women can be breadwinners and decide not to marry if they don't find the right partner. Parental resources also impact on men and women as does living at home with parents. While living at home with parents encourages marriage, moving out of the parental home delays marriage.

The unmarried population has increased among many groups, with the biggest changes characterizing Latinos and African Americans. Two reasons for this shift among Latinos are: 1) the Latino population is much younger than the non-Latino population, thus a higher percentage of Latinos have not yet reached an age appropriate for marriage, and 2) many of those migrating for economic reasons may be postponing marriage until they can support a family. For large numbers of African Americans who are postponing marriage, they may never marry. Both structural and personal attitudes are behind African American marital postponements and nonmarriage.

For older singles who want to marry or remarry, the double standard still favors men. Aging women are typically seen as "over the hill" whereas aging men are often described as "mature" and "distinguished." There's also a greater tendency to become choosier. At the same time there are fewer choices because the most desirable people are already married to other most desirable people. This section concludes with a discussion of the pros and cons that accompany a never-married status.

Several myths about singles exist, including that singles are tied to their mothers' apron strings; that they are selfish and self-centered; that they are well-off financially; that they are happier; and that there is something wrong with people who do not marry. Singlehood is not problem-free; the difficulties vary in terms of such variables as physical and emotional well-being (especially by gender), accessibility to housing, and age.

Cohabitation is a living arrangement in which two people who are not related and not married live together and usually have a sexual relationship. Cohabitants are sometimes called POSSLQs, meaning persons of the opposite sex sharing living quarters. The Census Bureau identifies cohabitating couples by counting unmarried-couple households. There are several types of cohabitation, with the most common being part-time/limited cohabitation, premarital cohabitation, and cohabitation that is a substitute for a legal marriage. Contrary to public image, cohabitation is not a college-student phenomenon; many

89

cohabitors have been divorced or have children in the home. Like other lifestyles, cohabitation has both advantages and disadvantages. Cohabitation does not necessarily lead to egalitarian gender roles, and several studies have suggested that women are frequently exploited economically as a result of cohabitative relationships. Most studies do not support the popular notion that cohabitation leads to better marriages. Unmarried couples have very little legal protection. Until laws are changed, unmarried couples are at a distinct disadvantage compared to married partners in terms of financial and legal rights. In contrast to the United States, policies in several other countries encourage, rather than impede, cohabitation (e.g. Sweden and Denmark).

Gay and lesbian households reflect another alternative lifestyle; just as there is no "typical" lifestyle for heterosexual singles, so there is no one lifestyle typical of homosexuals. There are several variations between the households of gay men and lesbians. Homosexual families are considered an alternative lifestyle because legal marriages between homosexual partners are banned by every state. Same-sex marriages aren't officially considered marriages but registered partnerships. Some states, however, have given gay and lesbian couples certain rights (e.g. adoption). Also, some corporations have started extending medical and other benefits to partners of gay and lesbian employees. On the other hand, President Clinton signed the Defense of Marriage Act in October 1996, which states that no U.S. state or territory has any legal duty to respect a marriage between homosexuals, even if such a marriage is valid in any other state. The Act also bans any form of federal aid to a married couple unless the couple is in "a legal union between one man and one woman as husband and wife." That would rule out any use in the future by a married homosexual couple of tax or other benefits tied to marriage.

Studies done thus far on children raised in homosexual households show no adverse effects, but some investigations report typical gender stereotyping; despite this, some therapists have strong reservations about the practice of raising children in homosexual families. Homosexual relationships have become more visible and more likely to be accepted than they once were, but homosexual households still face stigmas and problems that do not characterize nonmarried heterosexual relationships. One of the major problems for homosexual couples is job discrimination. Homosexuals face a variety of legal problems and it may take a long time for attitudes and laws to change.

Communes are collective households in which children and adults live together. There is a great deal of variation in the amount of sharing of economic, sexual, and decision-making rights within communes. Communal living arrangements have changed since the turn of the century and even since the 1970s. Communes are less numerous and less popular today, but they still fulfill some of the economic and social needs of many adults. Most communities have been short-lived, and communal living has attracted little recent interest from researchers. A growing number of elderly people are choosing to live in communal societies rather than moving in with their children or living in retirement or nursing homes.

CURRENT APPLICATIONS

1. Some observers are predicting that as we approach the end of the twentieth century, young men and women may be less inclined to postpone marriage, thus they will marry at an earlier age. These forecasters base their point of view on several social phenomena, including widespread alienation, feelings of loneliness, and the ever more threatening specter of AIDS. What do YOU think about these predictions? Compare your personal reactions with other members of the class. Try to integrate your thinking along these lines with the text's discussion of the pros and cons of singlehood.

2. The text observes that at present, no state within our country acknowledges legal marriage between homosexual partners. Obviously, there are strong religious prohibitions against homosexuality, and these help to explain America's attitudes toward homosexuality. But, one may ask, what is the "big deal" about homosexual marriage? Only homosexuals would be involved. What do heterosexuals have to fear, if anything, if homosexual marriage were made legal? Your critical thinking along these lines should help to expose some of the elements of America's *homophobia* (fear and hatred associated with homosexuality).

3. During the 1960s and 1970s, *communes* and *intentional communities* were "hot" topics, commanding considerable interest from social science researchers. As pointed out in Chapter Nine, sociologists who have studied communes indicate that "the modern communal movement is dead, or at least dormant." What happened to the communal movement? Think about how American values during the decades of the 60s and 70s were conducive to communes, in contrast to the values of the 80s and 90s. How has the conservative trend in the United States affected alternative lifestyles in general? What do you think the future holds for communes and other alternatives to conventional marriage and family lifestyles?

4. In recent years, there have been any numbers of articles in popular publications that deal with the phenomenon of "friends as family." In other words, it is becoming more common to find adult men and women who have decided to remain single *permanently,* and other than the members of their families of orientation, their "family" is made up of *friends* rather than spouses and dependent children. What do you think about this trend? Do you have any friends who have adopted this lifestyle? What do they have to say about it?

KEY TERMS FILL-IN

1. The _____ _____ is the term originally given to the situation resulting from the baby boom of the late 1940s to the early 1960s where a large number of women reached marriageable status only to find a scarcity of suitable partners.

2. _____ is a living arrangement in which two people who are not related and unmarried live together and usually have a sexual relationship.

3. Those who cohabit are called _____.

4. _____ cohabitation refers to a pattern of "drifting into cohabitation."

5. In _____ cohabitation, the couple is testing the relationship before making a final commitment.

6. A _____ _____ is a long-term commitment between two people without a legal marriage.

7. According to social scientists, those people likely to cohabit differ from those who do not in ways that predispose them to eventual divorce. This theory is called the _____ hypothesis.

MULTIPLE CHOICE

1. Because nearly _____ percent of all Americans eventually marry, marriage is still the norm.
   a. 52
   b. 63
   c. 78
   d. 93

2. _____ singles are open to marriage, but place a lower priority on searching for mates than on other activities, and sometimes the men and women in this group cohabit.
   a. Voluntary temporary
   b. Voluntary stable
   c. Involuntary stable
   d. Involuntary temporary

3. Those who have been married but do not want to remarry, those who are living together but do not intend to marry, and those whose lifestyles preclude the possibility of marriage, are classified as:
   a. voluntary temporary.
   b. voluntary stable.
   c. involuntary stable.
   d. involuntary temporary.

4. _____ singles include widowed, divorced, and single parents who would like to get married.
   a. Voluntary temporary
   b. Voluntary stable
   c. Involuntary stable
   d. Involuntary temporary

5. Singles who suffer from some physical or psychological impairment that prevents them from being successful in the marriage market are classified as:
   a. voluntary temporary.
   b. voluntary stable.
   c. involuntary stable.
   d. involuntary temporary.

6. In comparing women's and men's approaches to marriage:
   a. men are more likely than women to delay marriage.
   b. in their later years (over age 45), men are more likely than women to live alone.
   c. today, women are rushing into marriage for fear there will be no eligible men later on.
   d. some cite the marriage squeeze as the principal contributor to women's postponement of marriage.

7. The term _____ has been utilized in describing the situation resulting from the baby boom of the late 1940s and early 1960s wherein large numbers of women reached marriageable status only to find a scarcity of suitable partners.
   a. marriage squeeze
   b. marital bingo
   c. marriage-go-round
   d. spousal roulette

8. According to the text's discussion of Latinos:
   a. there has been far more research on Latino singles than on any other racial or ethnic minority group.
   b. Puerto Rican women tend to have more children out of wedlock than do either Mexican American or Cuban American women.
   c. Latino men seldom expect to marry although many of them do.
   d. the Cuban community has always de-emphasized the importance of marriage and children.

9. Which of the following is NOT one of the popular myths about singlehood mentioned in the text?
   a. Singles are tied to their mother's apron strings.
   b. Singles are selfish and self-centered.
   c. Singles are lonely and unhappy.
   d. There is something wrong with people who do not marry.

10. Most people define _____ as living together without being married.
    a. singlehood
    b. substitute marriage
    c. cohabitation
    d. communing

11. Cohabitants are sometimes called:
    a. singles
    b. POSSLQs
    c. homosexuals
    d. blended families

12. There is no long-term commitment in the _____ type of arrangement.
    a. premarital cohabitation
    b. communing
    c. part-time/limited cohabitation
    d. substitute marriage

13. For many people, _____ is a "new step between dating and marriage."
    a. premarital cohabitation
    b. communing
    c. part-time/limited cohabitation
    d. substitute marriage

14. In _____, one of the partners might be highly dependent and/or insecure and might prefer any kind of relationship to being alone.
    a. premarital cohabitation
    b. communing
    c. part-time/limited cohabitation
    d. substitute marriage

15. Most cohabiting relationships are relatively short-lived, with a median duration of:
    a. 6 months.
    b. one to two years.
    c. 15 to 18 months.
    d. two and one-half years.

16. _____ rates are higher for women than for men and most common for those with low socioeconomic status who grew up in broken homes or in families that depended on welfare.
    a. Cohabitation
    b. Singlehood
    c. Promiscuity
    d. Homosexuality

17. According to the text, about 36 percent of cohabiting homes include:
    a. aging parents.
    b. siblings.
    c. children under age 15.
    d. ex-spouses.

18. Which of the following is NOT one of the advantages of cohabitation cited in the text?
    a. It provides the emotional security of an intimate relationship but allows independence.
    b. It gives people the ability to avoid the sexual problems usually associated with marriage.
    c. It enables people to establish a meaningful relationship instead of participating in superficial dating games.
    d. It provides an opportunity to find out how much the partners really care about each other.

19. According to the text, cohabitation:
    a. promotes egalitarian gender roles.
    b. leads to better marriages.
    c. offers legal advantages not available to married couples.
    d. appears to lead to higher expectations for marriage than among other couples.

20. In Sweden, _____ percent of married couples live together before marriage.
    a. 65
    b. 71
    c. 80
    d. 99

21. The act signed in October 1996 by President Clinton which states that no U.S. state or territory has any legal duty to respect a marriage between homosexuals was the:
    a. Defense of Marriage Act.
    b. Gay Marriage Prohibition Act.
    c. Registered Partnership Act.
    d. Anti-Sodomy Act.

22. According to the text's discussion of gays and lesbians:
    a. most homosexuals are neurotic.
    b. gay and lesbian cohabitants rarely argue about previous lovers.
    c. homosexual partners rarely assume traditional breadwinner/homemaker roles.
    d. gay and lesbian relationships are almost always harmonious.

23. Kurdick (1994) found that all cohabitants, whether heterosexual or homosexual, experienced similar degrees of conflict in the area(s) of:
    a. power.
    b. personal flaws.
    c. intimacy.
    d. all of the above.

24. Some _____ permit individual ownership of private property; others do not.
    a. substitute marriages
    b. kibbutzim
    c. religious orders
    d. communes

25. In _____, there are strong emotional parent-child ties, and parents are very involved in the decision making concerning their child's future.
    a. hippie communes
    b. religious communes
    c. collective communities
    d. the Israeli kibbutz

ANSWERS

KEY TERMS FILL-IN

ANSWERS	PAGE NUMBERS
1. marriage squeeze	197
2. Cohabitation	203
3. POSSLQs	203
4. Part-time/limited	203
5. premarital	204
6. substitute marriage	204
7. selectivity or unconventionality	208

MULTIPLE CHOICE

ANSWERS	PAGE NUMBER
1. d	193

MARRIAGE AND COMMUNICATION IN INTIMATE RELATIONSHIPS

9

CHAPTER OBJECTIVES

Based upon their reading and careful consideration of Chapter Nine, students should:

1. understand why people marry.

2. be familiar with the marriage rituals in American society: engagement, shower and bachelor parties, and the wedding itself.

3. be able to describe the different types of marriages, including familiarity with the Cuber and Harroff typology, the research more recently conducted by Lavee and Olson (1993), and Wallerstein and Blakeslee (1995).

4. be able to identify the characteristics that typify a "successful marriage."

5. be familiar with the pros and cons of marriage contracts.

6. be familiar with the gender differences in terms of domestic work, including housework and child care.

7. understand the distinction between "his" and "her" marriages in terms of adjustment to married life, health and happiness, and equality in housework.

8. be able to identify those factors that are related to marital success and those that associate with marriage burnout.

9. understand how marriages change throughout the life cycle; be able to describe the five types of marriages across the life cycle, and be familiar with the major characteristics of each stage.

10.   understand the dynamics of power, conflict, and communication, including resource and exchange theories, types of power, and the reasons and remedies for conflict.

11.   be able to identify sex differences in communication.

12.   be able to identify the major barriers to marital communication patterns and the features of effective communication.

13.   be able to identify the most common sources of disagreements among couples.

14.   be aware of the most productive methods of dealing with conflict in a relationship.

CHAPTER OVERVIEW

While people marry for a variety of reasons, the single greatest attraction is the continuous and intimate companionship with a loved one. One of the keys to enduring intimate relationships is the ability to communicate effectively. Marriages tend to be short-lived if the relationship is based on myths and misinformation.

Marriage is a critical rite of passage in almost every culture. The major events that mark the beginning of a marriage are engagement, shower and bachelor parties, and the wedding itself. An engagement serves at least five functions. First, it sends a message to others to "keep their hands off" the future bride and bridegroom. Second, it gives both partners a chance to become better acquainted with future in-laws and to strengthen their identity as a couple. Third, it provides each partner with information about a prospective spouse's potential or current medical problems (e.g. through blood tests). Fourth, it legitimizes premarital counseling, particularly when they come from different backgrounds. Fifth, when a couple has been living together, the engagement signals the intent to make the union legal.

When it comes to the wedding itself, we see more men becoming involved in wedding preparations. For many who remarry, they want to involve their children in the ceremony. A discussion of marriage contracts points out both pros and cons; some of the arguments for and against marriage contracts are similar to those for and against cohabitation. Critics of contracts contend that they set a pessimistic tone for the marriage. It's also noted that marriage contracts aren't always binding in court, and if the contract is executed in a state other than where it was drawn up, the couple will experience legal problems. In addition, because people change over time, their original viewpoints may no longer be reflected in the contract.

Some couples write marriage contracts to avoid some forms of conflict and power struggles, at least economic issues. Despite various drawbacks associated with these arrangements, marriage contracts are becoming increasingly popular.

CHARACTERIZING MARRIAGES

There are different types of marriages. In their typology, Cuber and Harroff identified five types: conflict-habituated, devitalized, passive-congenial, vital, and total. Some were happy and some were not, but all endured. These researchers found that 80 percent of the marriages they studied fell into the first three categories and they characterized these as utilitarian marriages because they appeared to be based on convenience; the last two types were called intrinsic marriages because the relationships seemed to be inherently rewarding (vital marriages made up 15 percent of the sample, while total marriages accounted for only 5 percent.

A more recent study by Lavee and Olson reported more complexity and variety in marital relationship patterns, a similar picture was painted: 75 to 80 percent of marriages in their study were essentially based on convenience. Married singles are married partners who, by choice or necessity, live under the same roof, may be good friends, and may or may not have sexual intercourse but who have in many ways drifted apart because of conflicting work schedules, interests, personality differences, or other reasons.

Wallerstein and Blakeslee's (1995) survey of 50 white, middle-class, and well-educated couples who had been married nine years or longer identified four types of "good marriages." (Note that each type contained elements of "anti-marriage" which may strengthen or endanger the marriage. Their typology is comprised of the romantic marriage, the rescue marriage, the companionate marriage, and the traditional marriage.

MARITAL SUCCESS AND HAPPINESS

Because there is no generally agreed-upon definition, researchers describe the success or satisfaction of marriages based on the marital partners' own evaluations. Couples who say they are happy in their marriages have described three main ingredients: 1) each spouse must have a positive attitude toward the other and like the other as a person and a good friend; 2) both partners see marriage as a long-term commitment and a sacred institution in which the vow of "death 'till us part" is taken seriously and conflict is managed; and 3) happily married couples frequently say that providing emotional support is more important than romantic love. Benokraitis notes that, "In contrast, partners in unhappy marriages keep trying to change one another to fulfill their own needs and often become frustrated and angry when their efforts fail. The partners frequently react to one another when angry. Hostile, sarcastic criticism may lead to verbal or physical abuse. And, because people in unhappy marriages spend little time together, there is little chance their problems can be solved through discussion or by sharing common activities or day to day interaction." Unhappy marriages do not always end in divorce; the dissatisfaction, or marriage burnout, can go on for many years.

DOMESTIC LIFE

One of the most controversial issues is the equitable distribution of household and child-care tasks when both partners work outside the home. There seems to be a kind of self-fulfilling prophecy in terms of women assuming more responsibility for domestic chores than men: that women are "better suited" to these tasks. Men are doing slightly more and women slightly less housework than 30 years ago, but overall, women are still doing 80 percent of the traditional female jobs. The division of labor in this regard is affected by employment status, race and ethnicity, and social class. Men's lower participation in household tasks is usually, but not always, the result of long-accepted cultural views of men's and women's proper roles.

HOW MARRIAGES CHANGE THROUGHOUT THE LIFE CYCLE

All marriages change throughout the life cycle. At least five types of marriages can be described across the life cycle: first-year marriages, families with young children, families with adolescent children, middle-aged families, and families in later life. Life-cycle analyses must be evaluated in view of their limitations. In general, it may be observed from such analyses that the early years of marriage are particularly difficult for teenage couples; that having children decreases marital satisfaction temporarily; and that marital problems differ by social class, age, and the particular stage in the life cycle.

Men and women experience marriage differently. Some of these differences reflect the differential status of men and women in society, the organization of household work, and child-care responsibilities. Married couples go through identity bargaining and adjust through a process called *foreclosure.* There is a generally positive relationship between marriage and health, but being married does not automatically guarantee better health. A number of studies have found that, overall, married women are less healthy than are married men.

Power and conflict are normal and inevitable in close relationships, but effective communication can decrease power struggles and conflict that might lead to marital dissolution. Some scholars use resource theories to explain family structures and marital power. Resource theory can combine with exchange theory to explain the trade-offs husbands and wives often negotiate. There are different types of power. When couples fail to communicate, most of the ensuing conflict is related to such issues as gender differences, loyalty, money, power, sex, privacy, and children. Marital conflict is both common and normal. Marriages do not terminate because of conflict, but because of communication breakdown or failure to confront communication problems. Families use various techniques for ending conflict, including submission, compromise, standoff, and withdrawal. Family therapists and clinicians have developed many guidelines to help couples change and improve their communication patterns. Therapy and counseling may not always be successful, however, and communication failure is commonplace. An important first step in effective communication is self-disclosure. Disclosure is beneficial under four conditions of support: esteem, information, instrumental, and motivational. The most common behaviors related to ineffective marital communication are: not listening; not responding to the issue at hand; blaming, criticizing, nagging, and arguing; using scapegoats; using coercion and contempt; and using the silent treatment. According to researchers and practitioners, there are a number of ways to increase positive communication and decrease negative interaction patterns in marriage.

CURRENT APPLICATIONS

1. It doesn't take a rocket scientist to figure out that the value system of American society is more conservative today than it was two or three decades ago. Some observers are suggesting that there is a "back to the family" movement in progress, wherein Americans are becoming more inclined toward traditional values concerning marriage and family. One forecast is that young people may begin to marry earlier and that these young marrieds will be more likely to want to have children. Furthermore, the specter of AIDS may supercharge this trend toward earlier marriage, since the "safest" sex takes place between two partners who do not have the virus and who are faithful to each other sexually. Consider some of these issues in light of how you feel about marriage, having children, and other traditional family values.

103

2. Would you consider initiating a marriage contract? In your judgment, does such an agreement violate your perceptions of what a marriage should be? That is, if a couple sets up a marriage contract, aren't they really saying that they expect to eventually divorce? What, in your estimation, are the pros (if any) and cons of marriage contracts?

3. Evaluate your parents' marriage (and your own, if you are currently married) in terms of Cuber and Harroff's, Lavee and Olson's, and Wallerstein and Blakeslee's typologies. In doing this, recognize that any typology represents a *continuum*—a marriage may have characteristics of all the types that have been identified by these researchers. Furthermore, a marriage may change over time in terms of its predominant qualities. After you have performed this analysis, consider the question of whether it is necessarily "good" to have, say, a total or vital marriage, and whether it is necessarily "bad" to have, for example, a devitalized, passive-congenial, or conflict-habituated relationship.

4. The author of your textbook points out that self-disclosure is difficult for most people. Intellectually and philosophically this is pretty easy to accept; we are often unwilling to be open and honest with others, especially when it comes to those elements of our lives that we regard as the most personal. How much self-disclosure have *you* engaged in with others who are close to you? Be candid and honest, now...how open have you been? how many stones have been left unturned? Unless you are extremely unusual, there are some "secrets" that may never be revealed to *anyone*. Why not? Might your orientation be harmful to a current or future relationship? What makes you feel that way?

KEY TERMS FILL-IN

1. In the past an _____ was the last formal step of the courtship processes before marriage.

2. In a _____-_____ _____, the partners fight both physically and emotionally but do not believe that fighting is a reason for a divorce.

3. In a _____ _____, the partners are initially deeply in love when they marry, however, as time goes on activities become obligatory, done out of duty not joy.

104

4. In a _____-_____ _____ the couple marries with low emotional investments and expectations that remain constant.

5. In the _____ _____, the partner's lives are closely intertwined.

6. In the _____ _____, the partners participate in each other's lives at all levels and have few areas of tension or unresolved hostility.

7. _____ _____ are based on convenience.

8. In _____ _____, the relationships are inherently rewarding.

9. _____ _____ are married partners who, by choice or necessity, live under the same roof, may be good friends, and may or may not have sexual intercourse but who have in many ways drifted apart for any number of reasons.

10. Married couples go through _____ _____, during which they readjust their idealized expectations to the realities of married life.

11. _____ _____ is the gradual deterioration of love and ultimate loss of an emotional attachment between marital partners which can go on for many years.

12. Sociologists define _____ as the ability to impose one's will on others.

13. _____-_____ refers to "telling another about oneself, honestly offering one's thoughts and feelings for the other's perusal, and hoping that truly open communication will follow."

MULTIPLE CHOICE

1. Because many couples now cohabit before they get married,
   _____ is/are often more casual and informal.
   a. going steady
   b. engagements
   c. wedding plans
   d. honeymoons

2. In a _____ marriage, the subject of the controversy is
   insignificant, and the partners seldom resolve their disputes.
   a. devitalized
   b. passive-congenial
   c. conflict-habituated
   d. vital

3. Marriage contracts are drawn up for roughly _____
   percent of all remarriages.
   a. 5
   b. 10
   c. 15
   d. 20

4. In a _____ marriage, one or both partners may not be
   happy about the situation but both are resigned to it.
   a. devitalized
   b. passive-congenial
   c. conflict-habituated
   d. vital

5. _____ couples emphasize the practicality of the marriage
   over emotional intensity.
   a. Devitalized
   b. Passive-congenial
   c. Conflict-habituated
   d. Vital

6. When a disagreement occurs in a _____ marriage, it is
   over a specific issue and is quickly resolved.
   a. devitalized
   b. passive-congenial
   c. conflict-habituated
   d. vital

7. The _____ marriage is more all-encompassing than the vital marriage.
    a. devitalized
    b. passive-congenial
    c. conflict-habituated
    d. total

8. Couples who resolve conflict through compromise are classified as:
    a. vital.
    b. devitalized.
    c. passive-congenial.
    d. conflict-habituated.

9. Typical couples, who admit having problems, are given negative labels such as:
    a. utilitarian.
    b. devitalized.
    c. passive-congenial.
    d. conflict-habituated.

10. _____ are married partners who, by choice or necessity, live under the same roof, may be good friends, and may or may not have sexual intercourse but who have in many ways drifted apart because of conflicting work schedules.
    a. Passive congenials
    b. Harmonious couples
    c. Married singles
    d. Cohabiting partners

11. Wallerstein and Blakeslee called marriages in which passionate sex is an ongoing thing and the couples retain a "glow" over the years based on the belief that they were destined to be together the:
    a. romantic marriage.
    b. rescue marriage.
    c. compassionate marriage.
    d. traditional marriage.

12. The text describes five types of marriages across the life cycle. Which of the following is NOT one of these?
    a. the "sandwich" family
    b. the early years of marriage
    c. the middle-aged family
    d. the family in later life

13. Social scientists used to characterize middle-aged parents, particularly mothers, as experiencing *empty-nest syndrome,* but more recently, researchers have suggested that marital happiness and well-being:
    a. are completely arbitrary and unpredictable.
    b. follow a U-shaped curve.
    c. are bimodal in form.
    d. are curvilinear.

14. Couples who say they are happy in their marriages have described three main ingredients. Which of the following is NOT one of these?
    a. Each spouse must have a positive attitude toward the other.
    b. Both partners see marriage as a long-term commitment.
    c. Providing emotional support is more important than romantic love.
    d. Spouses must change one another to fulfill their own needs.

15. Who coined the phrase "his and her marriage"?
    a. John Cuber
    b. Nijole Benokraitis
    c. Jessie Bernard
    d. Willard Waller

16. In _____, couples negotiate adjustments to their new roles as husband and wife.
    a. foreclosure
    b. utilitarianism
    c. identity bargaining
    d. devitalization

17. When couples go through _____, it is typically the wife who accommodates the husband's needs.
    a. foreclosure
    b. utilitarianism
    c. identity bargaining
    d. devitalization

18. _____ might be characterized as the wife not even noticing that her husband falls asleep in the middle of her sentence.
    a. Primogeniture
    b. Marriage burnout
    c. Cross-complaining
    d. Scapegoating

19. A consistent finding in _____ research is that reciprocity is important if it is to be effective in communication and conflict resolution.
    a. self-summarizing
    b. self-disclosure
    c. cross-complaining
    d. counterproposal

20. In nonmarital relationships, males disclose more fully to females than to other males, probably because women are seen as:
    a. weak.
    b. motherly.
    c. nonthreatening.
    d. having less power.

21. Presenting one's own complaints without addressing the partner's complaints is:
    a. self-summarizing.
    b. counterproposals.
    c. cross-complaining.
    d. scapegoating.

22. Ignoring the partner's proposal for a solution and presenting one's own ideas is:
    a. self-summarizing.
    b. counterproposals.
    c. cross-complaining.
    d. scapegoating.

23. _____ is often an excuse to change our partners and not ourselves.
    a. Self-summarizing
    b. Counterproposals
    c. Cross-complaining
    d. Scapegoating

24. _____ is one of the most common behaviors that leads to anger and hostility in relationships.
    a. Using the silent treatment
    b. Cross-complaining
    c. Scapegoating
    d. Coercion

ANSWERS

KEY TERMS FILL-IN

ANSWERS	**PAGE NUMBERS**
1. engagement	216-217
2. conflict-habituated marriage	221
3. devitalized marriage	221
4. passive-congenial marriage	222
5. vital marriage	222
6. total marriage	222
7. Utilitarian marriages	222
8. intrinsic marriage	222
9. Married singles	222
10. identity bargaining	226
11. Marital burnout	228
12. power	238
13. Self-disclosure	234

MULTIPLE CHOICE

ANSWERS		**PAGE NUMBERS**
1.	b	218
2.	c	221
3.	d	221
4.	a	221
5.	b	222
6.	d	222
7.	d	222
8.	a	222
9.	b	223
10.	c	222
11.	a	224
12.	a	232-233
13.	b	233
14.	d	225
15.	c	226
16.	c	226
17.	a	226
18.	b	228-229

TO BE OR NOT TO BE A PARENT: MORE CHOICES, MORE CONSTRAINTS

10

CHAPTER OBJECTIVES

Based upon their reading and careful consideration of Chapter Ten, students should:

1. be able to discuss the costs and benefits of having children, reactions to pregnancy, and the effects of parenthood on mothers and fathers.

2. be familiar with the societal changes that affect parenthood, including alterations in fertility patterns.

3. be familiar with the reasons for postponing parenthood and the characteristics of older parents.

4. understand the reasons for infertility and the implications of involuntary childlessness for those who are involved.

5. understand the dynamics of becoming a parent despite infertility, including the circumstances surrounding adoption (including open and international adoption) and the benefits and liabilities of adoption.

6. be familiar with the different types of assisted reproductive techniques, including artificial insemination, fertility-enhancing drugs, in vitro fertilization (IVF), gamete intrafallopian transfer (GIFT), zygote intrafallopian transfer (ZIFT), embryo transplants, and surrogacy.

7. understand the benefits and risks of genetic engineering.

8. be familiar with the implications of having children outside of marriage, the characteristics of teenage parenting, and the individual/macro-level reasons for teenage pregnancy.

9. be familiar with the demographics of single parenthood and the different types of single parents.

10. be familiar with the reasons that men and women have for remaining childless.

11. understand the roles that contraception and abortion play in deciding not to parent, along with the surrounding controversies, and be familiar with the double standard in contraceptive practices.

12. be familiar with the process of abortion, the safety issues involved, attitudes toward abortion, and the globalization of the abortion debate.

13. be aware of the reasons why couples may choose to be child-free.

CHAPTER OVERVIEW

BECOMING A PARENT

Most couples have children because they really want them. Whether planned or not, a couple's first pregnancy is an important milestone. Cowan and Cowan (2000) have found four reaction patterns to the news of pregnancy: *planners, acceptance-of-fate couples, ambivalent couples,* and *yes-no couples.* As the ambivalence just described indicates, parenthood has both benefits and costs. Some of the advantages cited by both men and women are affection, close family ties, a feeling of immortality, and a sense of accomplishment. Among the costs: parenthood is expensive and there are emotional costs. Pregnancy can be exciting and a time of joy, but the experience is physically and emotionally demanding. Parenthood is steeped in romantic misconceptions and often we expect too much of mothers and ignore fathers. Many women experience postpartum depression. Fathers react in different ways to the birth process, including queasiness, a sense of increased responsibility, a fear of losing his spouse and/or child, and a feeling of vulnerability. Like mothers, fathers worry about being good parents. Fatherhood also enhances maturity. Married couples are not the only people who become parents.

FERTILITY PATTERNS IN THE UNITED STATES

There have been many changes in U.S. society since the early 1900s. Two of these changes that have had a major impact on parenthood are the decline in the fertility rate and the rising numbers of women in the labor force. One of the measures that demographers use to gauge population growth is the *fertility rate* (number of births per 1,000 women in their childbearing [ages 15-44] years). Much of the decrease in the overall fertility rate is attributable to macro-level social changes. Fertility rates vary considerably by race and ethnicity. These rates are higher for Hispanic-American women in comparison to non-Hispanic-American women, but there are intragroup variations, such as higher birthrates among Mexican-American women in comparison to Cuban-American women, due to socioeconomic differences.

POSTPONING PARENTHOOD

Women are beginning to postpone parenthood as well as marriage. Both individual-level and macro-level factors affect the decision to postpone parenthood. Older mothers tend to feel more self-assured, more ready for responsibility, and better-prepared for parenthood than younger women. There are some distinct drawbacks in deferred motherhood, however. Health risks are increased and practical liabilities are very real. Some women who have waited to have children find that it is too late to have as many children as they wanted. Mature mothers, especially those who have risen to powerful positions, may feel especially guilty about splitting time between their families and employers and "cheating" both. Men, on the other hand, who postpone parenthood usually enjoy more advantages and have fewer constraints than women as most men don't face gender discrimination in the workplace, they earn higher salaries, and have better health benefits. Thus, men are less likely to worry about not having the resources to raise children later in life. Also with more established careers, older fathers may have more flexibility to spend their non-work hours and weekends with their families.

INVOLUNTARY CHILDLESSNESS

Infertility is generally defined as the inability to conceive a baby after 12 months of unprotected sex. Infertility rates have remained fairly stable since the mid-1960s, but because more medical help is available, more couples are trying to circumvent this problem. Although infertility is attributable about equally to problems in males and females, until recently, most research on infertility focused on women. The two major causes of female infertility are failure to ovulate and blockage of the fallopian tubes. Another leading cause of infertility in women over 25 years of age is endometriosis. The rising incidence of infertility reflects not only female problems but also the fact that since the 1930s, male infertility, whose primary cause is a low sperm count, has become increasingly common. Chemical pollutants are believed to play a major role in male infertility. Not all scientists agree that the blame for male infertility lies in chemical pollutants, however. Some researchers maintain that, so far, there has been no conclusive evidence that low sperm counts result from environmental toxins.

BECOMING A PARENT DESPITE INFERTILITY

Adoption has been the traditional solution to infertility. When adoptions do take place today, they sometimes raise new issues. One such issue that has gained recent prominence is the nature and extent of the rights of biological fathers. Another controversial issue is transracial adoptions. Advocates for transracial adoption claim that many African-American or biracial children would remain in foster homes until age 18 if they weren't adopted by white families. There is also some evidence that when white adoptive families encourage children's participation in multicultural and multiracial activities, children in transracial adoptions have done well. Despite their findings that there is little difference in the self-concept or well-being between in-race and transracial adoptions, the National Association of Black Social Workers has strongly opposed transracial adoptions. A third controversial issue is open adoption. Many Americans have increasingly turned to international adoptions. National data show that, compared to children raised by never-married mothers, adopted children are economically advantaged. Some of the deterrents to adoption include societal beliefs that love and bonding in adoption are second best, that adoptive parents are simply not "real parents," and that adopted children are second-rate because of their unknown genetic past. The infertile couple now has many more options for having a child than before, but many assisted reproductive techniques are risky and success rates are not high. Assisted reproductive technologies like artificial insemination, fertility enhancing drugs, in vitro fertilization (IVF), gamete intrafallopian transfer (GIFT), zygote intrafallopian transfer (ZIFT), embryo transplants, and surrogacy have allowed many people to become parents despite infertility, but these techniques have generated a variety of legal, economic, social, and ethical concerns. Genetic research and biotechnology have been a blessing for many couples but some wonder if scientists are going too far. Among the controversial topics are amniocentesis, chronic villi sampling (CV), and BABI (blastomere analysis before implantation).

HAVING CHILDREN OUTSIDE OF MARRIAGE

Having children out of wedlock is not a recent phenomenon, but the percentages of such births have increased dramatically. Contrary to popular belief, unmarried teenagers have lower out-of-wedlock rates than older women, but these rates are rising among teens. The reasons for these high rates are complex; either individual, or micro-level, and structural, or macro-level, reasons interact. Among the individual reasons are misinformation about the relationship between sex and pregnancy; intentional pregnancy to satisfy emotional or status needs; rejection of abortion as an alternative; parental attitudes; and either misinformation about or lack of use of contraceptives. Structural reasons include socioeconomic factors, the media, and the fact that our society is so complex, there is little direct communication between individuals.

Childless couples are a minority, but remaining childless is becoming more acceptable. Women who expect to remain childless are more likely to be white, in their thirties, college educated, and career oriented. The major reason that couples give for remaining childfree is the freedom to achieve self-fulfillment. Childless couples say they are very happy. Improved contraceptive techniques have resulted in fewer unwanted births. The only foolproof contraceptive, however, is abstinence. There is a "double standard" involved with contraception: it is a woman's problem/responsibility. Nearly 60 percent of couples throughout the world practice contraception. Abortion is the expulsion of the embryo or fetus from the uterus. It can occur naturally—as in a spontaneous abortion, or miscarriage—or it can be induced medically. The number of abortions performed in the United States dropped from 1.6 million in 1990 to 1.2 million in 1996; some reasons for this decrease include the greater use of condoms because of the fear of AIDS; the decision by more single women to keep their babies; and the pressure exerted by anti-abortion activists on small hospitals to stop performing abortions. Safety can be measured on two levels: physical and emotional. There is ongoing conflict between abortion proponents and opponents, and there is even some question about whether the nation as a whole agrees with the current regulated legality of abortion. Pro-life organizations have accelerated their efforts and the future legal admissibility of abortive techniques is uncertain.

DECIDING TO BE CHILDFREE

Women who expect to remain childfree are more likely to be white, in their 30s, college educated, and career oriented. They tend to have greater aspirations for upward mobility than other women, to be less willing to accept the role of "homemaker," and plan to marry at a later age than other women. The major reason why couples remain childless is the freedom to do what they want; this freedom may be one of the reasons childless couples say they are very happy.

CURRENT APPLICATIONS

1. As pointed out in Chapter 10, many people have children because they really want them, but at least half of all pregnancies are unintended and over one-third are ill-timed. One strategy for understanding the effects of unwanted or ill-timed pregnancy is to compare this situation to other life circumstances involving unanticipated responsibilities and expenditures. It has been estimated that the "lifetime" costs to the average parent, per child, ranges into the hundreds of thousands of dollars. Most adults know what it is like to think about buying a new car. How many times have you heard people agonize over "whether they want to have a new car payment in their budgets." "Gee, I would like to have a new car, and I've been looking at them over the past few days, and I think I'm suffering from 'sticker shock.'" Even the most expensive new cars usually cost no more than $50,000. Having a child incurs four or five times this amount over a twenty-five year period. Thought about in this way, one can clearly see how expensive having children can be. Yet, do you think that most people consider parenthood in these terms? If not, make a list of the reasons why not.

2. Sex determination continues to be a controversial social issue, and as techniques become more sophisticated, the possibility of predicting the sex of an infant before birth becomes more real for American couples. Research shows that Americans continue to have a preference for male children. Think about what would happen if our society had an abundance of males, but not enough females. Do you think this is a real possibility? Why or why not?

3. The United States is an extremely child- and parent-focused society. In order to illustrate for yourself how powerful the motivations to become a parent are in American society, orchestrate the following scenario: Engage one or more of your friends (not taking this course) in a conversation about the pros and cons of having children. Then, deliberately take the point of view that *remaining childless* is a viable option for you personally. If you feel you can "afford" to go this far, suggest to this person (or persons) that you are not, in fact, particularly fond of children in the first place...that there are many other activities that you are more interested in. Obviously, there is some potential for friction here, but if you can persevere, this will be an excellent real-life illustration of how much pressure Americans feel to parent.

4. Statistics about adopting children in the United States can be very confusing. On the surface, it appears that it is extremely difficult

to adopt a child. In fact, the difficult part is finding a "blonde-haired, blue-eyed" child. In other words, prospective parents are most particular about the characteristics of the children they intend to adopt. What is your personal point of view? Suppose you have just learned that you cannot have biological children and you want to adopt. Would you be content to adopt a child who is a member of an ethnic or racial group other than your own? Would you be willing to adopt a child whose biological parents were impoverished, uneducated, and long-time welfare recipients? Why or why not?

KEY TERMS FILL-IN

1. Chronic drinking during pregnancy may lead to _____ _____ _____.

2. Many women experience _____ _____ after the birth of the baby.

3. The _____ rate is the number of births per 1,000 women in their childbearing years.

4. _____ is generally defined as an inability to conceive after 12 months of unprotected sex.

5. _____ _____ _____ can produce scarring that blocks the fallopian tubes.

6. The greatest cause of the rise of pelvic inflammatory disease is the massive spread of _____.

7. _____ is another leading cause of infertility in women over 25 years of age.

8. _____ _____ refers to the practice of sharing information and contact between biological and adoptive parents both during the adoption process and during the child's life.

9. _____ _____ refers to placing semen in the vagina or uterus by a means other than sexual intercourse.

10. _____ _____ _____ is a process that involves surgically removing eggs from a woman's ovaries, fertilizing them in a petri dish with sperm from her husband or another donor, and then reimplanting them in her uterus.

11. _____ _____ _____ is a procedure used to increase the chances that the fertilized egg will implant in the uterus wall, as doctors place both egg and sperm into the fallopian tube through a small incision in the woman's abdomen.

12. A procedure in which the wife's eggs are fertilized by her husband's sperm in vitro and are then transferred to the fallopian tube is called _____ _____ _____ .

13. For about $10,000 for each attempt, a fertilized egg can be implanted into an infertile woman. This technology is known as _____ _____.

14. In _____ a woman who is capable of carrying pregnancy to term serves as a surrogate mother for a woman who cannot bear children.

15. _____ is one of the prenatal screening procedures that is used to analyze genetic disorders and biochemical abnormalities in the fetus.

16. _____ _____ _____ can provide the same information as amniocentesis, but the information can be produced at ten weeks rather than 20 weeks into the pregnancy.

17. _____ is the prevention of pregnancy by behavioral, mechanical, or chemical means.

18. The natural expulsion of the embryo or fetus from the uterus is known as a spontaneous _____.

MULTIPLE CHOICE

1. Researchers Cowan and Cowan found four distinct reaction patterns to couples' reactions to the news of pregnancy. Which of the following is NOT one of these?
   a.   planning couples
   b.   acceptance-of-fate couples
   c.   incredulous couples
   d.   yes-no couples

2. Which of the following is NOT one of the benefits of having children cited in the text?
   a. freedom from emotional problems
   b. affection
   c. close family ties
   d. a feeling of immortality

3. _____ may be the result of sudden drops in levels of estrogen and progesterone because they are expelled with the placenta as the afterbirth.
   a. Beta-endorphins
   b. Idiopathic infertility
   c. pelvic inflammatory disease
   d. Postpartum depression

4. When _____ levels drop after birth, the mother may "crash," contributing to the postpartum depression.
   a. lactation
   b. testosterone
   c. beta-endorphins
   d. alpha-endorphins

5. Which of the following is NOT one of the fears and concerns of expectant and recent fathers, as cited by Shapiro?
   a. anxiety over whether the child will be attractive and intelligent
   b. increased responsibility
   c. queasiness
   d. uncertain paternity

6. _____ is generally defined as the inability to conceive a baby after twelve months of unprotected sex.
   a. Infertility
   b. Impaired fecundity
   c. PID
   d. ZIFT

7. Blockage of the _____ can cause infertility.
   a. endometrium
   b. uterus
   c. fallopian tubes
   d. vagina

8. The primary cause of male infertility is a low:
   a. sperm count.
   b. sex drive.
   c. sexual activity.
   d. seminal fluid.

9. _____ means that doctors just do not know what is wrong.
   a. Impaired fecundity
   b. Intermarital infertility
   c. Idiopathic infertility
   d. Zygote infertility

10. *Open adoption* refers to the practice of:
   a. allowing men and women of any racial or ethnic background the opportunity to adopt any child.
   b. sharing information and contact between biological and adoptive parents both during the adoption process and during the child's life.
   c. permitting the child to participate in the process of parent selection.
   d. taking the rights of fathers into account.

11. In the United States, the waiting period required to adopt a child is seven to ten years. Americans have increasingly turned to _____ adoptions.
   a. transracial
   b. biracial
   c. nondomestic
   d. international

12. Artificial insemination was first performed in
   a. the 1970s
   b. 1850.
   c. 1910.
   d. the 1790s.

13. Louise Brown, the first in vitro baby, was born in England in
   a. 1978.
   b. 1985.
   c. 1989.
   d. 1991.

14. More than one egg is usually implanted in the in vitro fertilization procedure in order to increase the chances of success, and nearly _____ of all women using in vitro procedures have multiple births.
    a. one-eighth
    b. one-quarter
    c. one-third
    d. one-half

15. *Pergonal* is a drug that:
    a. enhances women's fertility.
    b. enhances male fertility.
    c. elevates the human sex drive.
    d. mellows people's disposition about sex.

16. There have been three recent variations in the in vitro fertilization procedure. Which of the following is NOT one of these?
    a. gamete intrafallopian transfer (GIFT)
    b. intrauterine fertilization procedure (IFP)
    c. zygote intrafallopian transfer (ZIFT)
    d. intracytoplasmic sperm injection (ICSI)

17. In _____, the children are genetically unrelated to the mothers who bear them.
    a. gamete intrafallopian transfer
    b. zygote intrafallopian transfer
    c. embryo transplant
    d. artificial insemination

18. _____ provides information about the fetus' sex.
    a. Amniocentesis
    b. PID
    c. GIFT
    d. ZIFT

19. A troubling issue raised by embryo transplant technology is:
    a. that the resulting children are genetically unrelated to the mothers who bear them.
    b. that there is a question of ownership of embryos.
    c. what to do with the "leftovers."
    d. All of the above are issues raised by embryo transplant technology.

20. According to the text's discussion of out-of-wedlock birthrates,
    a. unmarried teenagers have the highest rates.
    b. unmarried teenagers have lower rates than older women.
    c. the rate of out-of-wedlock births is declining among teenagers.
    d. middle-aged women have higher rates than teenagers and older women combined.

21. According to the text, the major reason that couples remain childfree is:
    a. the financial expense.
    b. inertia.
    c. the freedom to do what they want.
    d. increased public acceptance of childlessness among married couples.

22. The Supreme Court decision that legalized abortion in the U.S. that decision was:
    a. *Roe v. Wade.*
    b. *NARL v. Connecticut.*
    c. *Sullivan v. Collingsworth.*
    d. *NOW (The National Organization of Women) v. New Jersey.*

23. Abortion is most common among women who are:
    a. middle-aged.
    b. Hispanic.
    c. teenagers.
    d. unmarried.

24. By 1992, the proportion of American couples who planned not to have children had reached _____ percent.
    a. 7
    b. 15
    c. 27
    d. 35

25. Which of the following is a true statement?
    a. China has had little success, to date, providing contraceptive information and technology to its people.
    b. Most families in China obtain exemptions from family size restrictions imposed by the government.
    c. Since 1979, China has maintained a strict policy of one child per family in order to limit the country's rapid population growth.
    d. While all levels of government in China have imposed strict fines and punishments on those who violate family size restrictions, none have offered incentives to observe these regulations.

ANSWERS

KEY TERMS FILL-IN

ANSWERS	PAGE NUMBERS
1. fetal alcohol syndrome	248
2. postpartum depression	248
3. fertility	249
4. Infertility	252
5. Pelvic Inflammatory Disease (PID)	252
6. chlamydia	252
7. Endometriosis	252
8. Open adoption	256
9. Artificial insemination	258
10. In vitro fertilization (IVF)	259
11. gamete intrafallopian transfer (GIFT)	259
12. zygote intrafallopian transfer (ZIFT)	259
13. embryo transplant	260
14. surrogacy	262
15. Amniocentesis	263
16. Chorionic villus sampling	263
17. contraception	266
18. abortion	268

MULTIPLE CHOICE

ANSWERS		PAGE NUMBERS
1.	c	245-246
2.	a	246
3.	d	248
4.	c	248
5.	a	249
6.	a	252
7.	c	252
8.	a	253
9.	c	253
10.	b	256
11.	d	256
12.	a	258
13.	a	259
14.	d	259
15.	a	259
16.	b	260
17.	c	260
18.	a	263
19.	d	264
20.	b	265
21.	c	271
22.	a	268
23.	d	268
24.	a	270-271
25.	c	267

RAISING CHILDREN: PROSPECTS AND PITFALLS

CHAPTER OBJECTIVES

Based upon their reading and careful consideration of Chapter Eleven, students should:

1.   understand how parental roles are learned.

2.   understand how infants affect parents.

3.   be able to discuss motherhood and fatherhood in terms of role theory.

4.   understand the characteristics of the parent-child relationship and be familiar with the theories of human development discussed in the text.

5.   be able to identify the popular myths associated with parenthood.

6.   be familiar with the prevailing research on only children.

7.   understand the implications of parenting the crowded "empty nest."

8.   be familiar with the "boomerang generation" and the complexities of relations between parents and adult children.

9.   be familiar with the three different parenting styles (authoritarian, permissive, and authoritative) and the eight different parental roles (martyr, pal, police officer, teacher, booster/promoter, designer, mediator, and supervisor).

10.   be aware of the variation in acceptable disciplinary measures across racial and ethnic lines.

11.   be able to identify the "inner resources" children need to become responsible adults.

12.   be prepared to discuss the consequences of limited parental time with children, including the phenomenon of latchkey children and the implications of child/day care.

13.   be able to compare and contrast homosexuals and heterosexuals in terms of parenting styles, disclosure, and acceptance.

14.   understand the reasons for the increasing rates of childhood poverty and be able to discuss the potential consequences in the future.

15.   be familiar with the characteristics and problems associated with foster homes.

CHAPTER OVERVIEW

CHANGING PARENTAL ROLES

Children affect adults long before they are born. Socialization is a reciprocal process, and infants are not passive participants, but rather play an active role in the socialization process. Contrary to popular belief, parenting does not come naturally and many parents do not realize that expecting a baby is very different from having one. The first year of parenting can be very demanding, as infants require "continuous coverage." To meet their child's survival needs, new parents must accept multiple roles. Parents' own activities are also altered as the workload increases, parents have less time for each other. Still, while couples may experience role strain, relationships can become richer.

Sociologists often use role theory to explain the interaction between family members. Despite the universality of parenthood, many mothers and fathers experience problems in their roles as parents. New mothers face enormous pressures. Fathers are more involved in childcare and housework than they were a generation ago, but the increases are modest. Still, they experience pressures as well. Many parents experience problems in raising children because they have unrealistic expectations, they believe many myths about child rearing, and they face greater pressures in balancing work and home responsibilities. Contemporary parenting roles are affected by parents being faced with increasing responsibility but less authority. Also, parents often experience role strain when they are judged by professionals rather than peers, and this makes many parents feel insecure and guilty. Note also, that parents have no training for their difficult role, yet they must live up to high standards.

New mothers often face enormous pressures because of the expectation that mothering "comes naturally." It assumes that a good mother will be perfect if she simply follows her instincts. It also implies that there is something wrong with a mother who doesn't devote 100 percent of her time to child rearing. It may also discourage the involvement of other adults, such as fathers or other caretakers.

Fathers, too, may feel role strain. In addition, they may have little opportunity to learn necessary parenting skills, especially during the baby's first year of life. Fathers play an important role in a child's emotional, social, and intellectual development. Gerson (1997) divides fathers into three types: breadwinner fathers, autonomous fathers, and involved fathers. The father-as-breadwinner model continues to be dominant today.

PARENTING ACROSS THE LIFE CYCLE

Most parents play a major role in their children's lives until the children reach early adulthood. Parents influence their children's development in different ways. There are different theories of human development, including Mead's theory of the social self, Piaget's cognitive development theory, and Erikson's psychosocial theory of development. Most people learn about child rearing from parents, friends, relatives, self-help books and even television talk shows. There are a variety of myths surrounding children, based upon some of these sources: 1) You can tell in infancy how bright a child is likely to be later on; 2) The more stimulation a baby gets, the better; 3) If a baby cries every time the mother leaves, it's an early sign of emotional insecurity; 4) Special talents surface early or not at all; 5) An only child is likely to have problems relating to others; 6) Children who suffer early neglect and deprivation will not realize their normal potential; and 7) Parental conflicts do not affect very young children. All of these myths reflect considerable misinformation about the child's early years.

A good parent-child relationship may change suddenly during adolescence. Many adolescents come from divorced families and are reared by single parents. In general, adolescent girls find the transition to puberty more difficult than boys do. Because of the awkward nature of this period of life, parenting adolescents can be difficult. The text also discusses gender differences in parenting as well as racial-ethnic variations in parenting.

Despite widespread beliefs that an only child is disadvantaged, there is no hard evidence to support this view. While only children do sometimes wish they had siblings and may also feel "it's easier for two kids to argue against parents," several studies have found that for the most part, "onlies" are not very different from children who grow up with

128

siblings. If anything, "onlies" are often more successful; this may be due largely to financial resources. When birth order is studied in terms of its effect on personality, the research to date remains inconclusive.

More young adults are living at home longer, and many of them who have left home frequently come back (the boomerang generation); this can present a variety of problems for the relationship between parents and adult children.

PARENTING STYLES AND DISCIPLINE

Parenting styles differ. Parents typically stress either autonomy or obedience. These opposing values are reflected in three basic approaches to child rearing: *Authoritarian* parents tend to be working class, expect absolute obedience from their children, and often use punitive measures to control behavior. Middle-class parents are usually *permissive*, valuing a child's freedom of expression, autonomy, and internal control, and using reason rather than overt power to accomplish their ends. *Authoritative* parents also encourage autonomy and self-reliance, but they tend to use positive reinforcement and avoid punitive, repressive discipline. Although parental roles overlap in the real world, there are eight identifiable styles: Parental roles that shape the child directly include the martyr, the pal or buddy, the police officer or drill sergeant, the teacher, and the booster or promoter. Other parenting strategies include "managing" children's social development by influencing their social environments and their interactions with peers; these approaches include the designer, the mediator, and the supervisor.

After a discussion of physical punishment as a method of discipline and variations in acceptable disciplinary measures across racial and ethnic lines, three types of "inner resources" children need to become responsible adults are noted. They are: 1) good feelings about themselves and others; 2) an understanding of right and wrong, and 3) alternatives for solving problems. Benokraitis concludes that effective discipline includes more than punishments. The most powerful parenting approaches include such activities as joint decision making between parents and children (especially adolescents), consistent parenting, and creating special times together.

Although children today spend less time with parents than children did in the past, parents are still the primary socialization agents. Many of the ideas parents have about child development are rooted in myth rather than reality and reflect much of our misinformation about the child's early years. Parents and children often want different things from each other. Whereas parents want adolescents to be more self-disciplined, obedient, and industrious, many adolescents want more independence and less responsibility.

NONPARENTAL CHILD CARE

Because both mothers and fathers work more hours to provide for their families today, there is less time for nurturing children. Parents often spend little time with their children because of shift work and employment demands. One result has been increased parenting by day-care centers. There are more absentee fathers today. Latchkey children have also become a growing concern. And childcare is also a controversial issue, although few studies have found that day-care has pronounced negative consequences. Nevertheless, day-care continues to be a controversial issue.

GAY AND LESBIAN PARENTS AND CHILDREN

In most cases, homosexual parenting is similar to heterosexual parenting. Some homosexual parents feel more pressure to be successful because they fear that they will lose visitation or custody rights. Children are usually accepting of homosexual parents, but society's homophobia may make it difficult for children to manage the knowledge of their parent's homosexuality outside of the immediate family or gay social contexts. Despite such concerns, there is no evidence that living with a homosexual parent has negative effects on children.

Anecdotal data suggests that many heterosexual parents have a problem accepting their children's homosexuality. Many parental reactions are initially negative because parents think that their children could be heterosexual if they wanted. Parents may also be concerned about being stigmatized themselves. Many conservatives, religious groups, and others reject the notion that gay and lesbian relationships are "normal." Recently, however, American Roman Catholic bishops issued a pastoral letter that advised parents of gay children to put love and support for their children before church doctrine that condemns homosexual activity.

CURRENT SOCIAL ISSUES ON CHIDREN'S WELL-BEING

According to the Census Bureau (U.S. Bureau of the Census, 1997) six of the most important risk factors between 1970 and 1996 were poverty, welfare dependence, absent parents, one-parent families, unwed mothers, and parents who did not graduate from high school. While many people overcome these obstacles, others do not. It is also noted that the risk factors are interrelated.

Increased poverty, child abuse, and parental neglect has resulted in increased out-of-home placements for children, including foster care, care by relatives, hospitalization, residential treatment facilities, group homes, and shelters for runaways. The most common out-of-home placement is the foster home, where a family raises children who are not its own for a period of time but does not formally adopt them. While foster homes are supposed to provide short-term care until the children can be adopted or returned to their biological parents, in reality, many children go through multiple placements and remain in foster care until late adolescence. The typical foster mother is paid very little and cares for a child who no one else is able to love or parent. While some children are closer to their foster families than their biological parents and prefer to live with their foster parents, others aren't able to adjust to their foster home. If children have experienced more than one or two placements and have been in foster care for more than a few years, their self-esteem, self-confidence and ability to establish satisfying relationships with peers may erode.

CURRENT APPLICATIONS

1. What style of parenting did your mother and father utilize in their relationship with you—authoritarian, permissive, or authoritative? If you have or plan to have children of your own, do you plan to utilize the same style? A different approach? Why? Of the five parental roles described (martyr, pal/buddy, police office/drill sergeant, teacher, or booster/promoter), which role did your parents play? Again, have you, or do you, anticipate playing the same role with your own children? A different role? Why?

2. Using Erikson's psychosocial theory, trace your own development through the stages in this paradigm. Utilize the outcome to try to interpret the difficulties you have experienced in growing up.

3. The "crowded empty nest" syndrome is being more commonplace today for adult children and their parents. One reality that more adult Americans are likely to experience involves what some have referred to as the "sandwich generation." This refers to parents who, at a time in their lives when they are beginning to look forward to freedom from responsibility for caring for their children, not only end up once again helping to support their adult children, but also feel obligated to take care of their own parents, who have become infirm. Whether you have had any personal experience playing one or more of these roles, think about what it would be like to be in a similar situation, either as the parent who assumes

the responsibility, the adult child who has "come home again," or the elderly mother or father who becomes dependent on his or her children.

4. What is your personal reaction to the phenomenon of *latchkey kids*? Do you think this is a problem? The *Home Alone* movies have made millions finding humor in this phenomenon (admittedly at an extreme). Are the "experts" exaggerating the severity of this problem? What do you think is the future of childcare in American society?

KEY TERMS FILL-IN

1. Gerson referred to fathers who view fatherhood mainly in economic terms and prefer a wife who is responsible for domestic responsibilities and childcare as _____ fathers.

2. Gerson would categorize a "deadbeat dad" who doesn't provide economic or emotional support after a marital breakup as an _____ father.

3. Although these fathers don't necessarily have equally shared or primary relationships with women and children, they do believe that "good fathering" includes extensive participation in the daily tasks of child rearing and nurturing. Gerson called them _____ fathers.

4. Young adults who move back with their parents after living independently for a while are called the _____ generation.

5. Diane Baumrind found that _____ approach parents tend to be working class and teach their children to respect authority, work, order, and traditional structure.

6. Middle-class parents use an approach to parenting that places a high value on children's freedom of expression and autonomy. Diana Baumrind called this approach to parenting the _____ approach.

7. _____ parents also encourage autonomy and self-reliance, but they tend to use positive reinforcement and to avoid punitive, repressive discipline.

8. The phrase _____ _____ is generally used to describe children who return home after school and let themselves in, with their own keys, to an empty house or apartment.

9. Families in which both parents are employed full time outside the home are referred to as _____.

10. The most common out-of-home placement for children is the _____.

MULTIPLE CHOICE

1. According to the text's discussion of learning parental roles:
   a. contrary to popular belief, parenting does *not* come naturally.
   b. most parents appreciate that expecting a baby is very different from having a baby.
   c. marriage relationships never become richer as a result of having children.
   d. babies are passive recipients of care rather than active participants in their own socialization.

2. Which of the following is true about contemporary parenting roles?
   a. Parenthood changes both partners on an individual level.
   b. Parents are faced with increasing responsibility but less authority.
   c. Parents frequently experience role strain.
   d. All of the above are true statements.

3. Today, the percentage of mothers who are in the workforce and have children under 18 years of age is:
   a. 33 percent.
   b. 44 percent.
   c. 58 percent
   d. over 70 percent.

4. Which is true about mothers in the U.S. today?
    a. Because nothing is a "natural" role, instincts alone insure effective role-playing.
    b. There is substantial evidence that mothers who are employed full-time are largely to blame for adolescent problems, preschool misbehavior, and difficulties in school.
    c. The greater the participation of the father in child-rearing, the greater the mother's satisfaction with parenting and marriage.
    d. All of the above are true.

5. Fathers play an important role in a child's _____ development.
    a. emotional
    b. social
    c. intellectual
    d. All of the above are true.

6. Which of the following is true of American fathers today?
    a. Fathers in middle-class families are more involved in child-care than lower income fathers.
    b. Constructive paternal involvement can help the mother become a better parent and benefits the marital relationship as well as the child's development.
    c. Fathers are more likely to provide care if they work the same shift week-in and week-out.
    d. All of the above are true statements.

7. Using Gerson's father typology, fathers who felt that "good fathering" includes extensive participation in the daily tasks of child rearing and nurturing were categorized as _____ fathers.
    a. breadwinner
    b. autonomous
    c. involved
    d. consummate

8. Gerson contended that _____ fathers seek freedom from family commitments and distance themselves – usually after a marital breakup from both their former spouses and children.
    a. autonomous
    b. absentee
    c. noninvolved
    d. punitive

9. _____ described psychosocial development as a passage through eight stages during the life cycle.
   a. Sigmund Freud
   b. Erik Erikson
   c. Emile Durkheim
   d. Abraham Maslow

10. During the _____ stage of Piaget's cognitive development theory, the child is self-centered and has difficulty taking another person's point of view.
   a. concrete
   b. sensorimotor
   c. formal operational
   d. preoperational

11. When the child can imagine alternatives to real-life situations; and to formulate creative solutions for problems, the child has reached what cognitive developmental theorist Jean Piaget termed the _____ stage.
   a. concrete
   b. sensorimotor
   c. formal operational
   d. preoperational

12. _____'s theory of human development is one of the few to extend to middle age and the later years.
   a. Erik Erikson
   b. George Herbert Mead
   c. Jean Piaget
   d. Carol Gilligan

13. In each of the developmental stages proposed by _____, the growing person faces a specific challenge that presents both opportunity and danger; the outcome of these "crises" determines whether the person will move on successfully to the next stage.
   a. George Herbert Mead
   b. Erik Erikson
   c. Jean Piaget
   d. Harry Harlow

14. Which of the following is NOT one of the myths about child development that is presented in your text?
    a. A child's intelligence can be determined in infancy.
    b. The more stimulation a baby gets, the better.
    c. Parental conflicts do not affect very young children.
    d. Only children tend to be somewhat less eager for social intimacy.

15. According to the text's discussion of adolescence,
    a. parent-child relationships rarely change during this period of development.
    b. parents differ very little in their relationships with their children.
    c. in general, adolescent girls find the transition to puberty more difficult than boys do.
    d. both teenagers and their parents report that most arguments are over major issues like what the youngsters will do with their future.

16. _____ parents teach their children to respect authority, work, order, and traditional structure.
    a. Authoritative
    b. Authoritarian
    c. Permissive
    d. Pessimistic

17. _____ parents set boundaries, but they are more subtle.
    a. Authoritative
    b. Authoritarian
    c. Permissive
    d. Pessimistic

18. _____ parents expect disciplined conformity.
    a. Authoritative
    b. Authoritarian
    c. Permissive
    d. Pessimistic

19. The text cities five parenting styles that influence the child directly. Which of the following is NOT one of these?
    a. the parent as martyr
    b. the parent as pal or buddy
    c. the parent as booster or promoter
    d. the parent as counselor

20. The text cites three parenting styles that shape the child's environment. Which of the following is NOT one of these?
    a. the parent as teacher
    b. the parent as designer
    c. the parent as mediator
    d. the parent as supervisor

21. Which of the following is NOT one of the values reflecting the Japanese approach to parenting?
    a. loyalty
    b. individualism
    c. obedience
    d. respect for authority

22. Japanese child rearing is based on a concept called *amae*, which is a sense of :
    a. independence based on individual autonomy.
    b. deference based on ultimate parental power.
    c. complete dependence based on the desire for love and caring.
    d. personal success based on self-reliance.

23. Many researchers and practitioners have agreed that physical punishment ineffective:
    a. as a punishment.
    b. for learning self-control.
    c. as a disciplinary method.
    d. for problem solving.

24. The text cites a variety of reasons why parents are discouraged from spanking or hitting their children. Which of the following is NOT one of these?
    a. Physical punishment has been proven to be totally ineffective in obtaining obedience.
    b. Children learn best by modeling their parents.
    c. Unexpressed anger is stored inside and may explode later.
    d. Physical punishment deprives the child of opportunities for learning effective problem solving.

25. The text cites three types of "inner resources" that children need if they are to become responsible adults. Which of the following is NOT one of these?
    a. good feelings about themselves and others
    b. an understanding of right and wrong
    c. a high degree of intelligence
    d. alternatives for solving problems

26. According to the text's discussion of what parents and children want from each other,
    a. the generation gap is a new phenomenon.
    b. one important reason for the generation gap is that parents and children often have different expectations.
    c. in terms of values, most parental expectations have changed dramatically over the years.
    d. since the 1950s, parents have said that the most important quality they value in their children is the willingness to be obedient.

27. Children who return home after school to an empty house or apartment, where they are alone and unsupervised until their parents or another adult comes home, are often referred to as:
    a. "home alone kids."
    b. psychologically abandoned.
    c. emotionally deprived.
    d. latchkey kids.

28. In _____ homes, families raise children who are not their own for a period of time without formal adoption.
    a. group
    b. foster
    c. juvenile
    a. community

29. According to the text's discussion of gay and lesbian parents:
    a. in most respects, lesbian and gay families are very different from heterosexual families.
    b. despite the anxiety of some homosexual parents, many children are generally accepting of gay or lesbian parents.
    c. anecdotal data suggest that most heterosexual parents have no problem accepting their children's homosexuality.
    d. all of the above

ANSWERS

KEY TERMS FILL-IN

ANSWERS   **PAGE NUMBERS**

1.   breadwinner   278

MULTIPLE CHOICE

12

RACIAL AND ETHNIC FAMILIES: STRENGTHS AND STRESSES

CHAPTER OBJECTIVES

Based upon their reading and careful consideration of Chapter Twelve students should:

1.　have an appreciation for the increasing diversity of American families.

2.　be familiar with the influx of immigrants to American society, the significance of minority groups, and the characteristics of racial-ethnic groups.

3.　be familiar with the structure of African American families, including the economic factors affecting these groups, the characteristics of husband-wife and parent-child relationships, the extended family focus, and the strengths of the African American family.

4.　be able to describe the family-related characteristics of American Indians and the changes and constraints in the American Indian family structure.

5.　be able to describe the characteristics of Latino families, understand familism as a value, be familiar with the extended family in Latino families, and be acquainted with the issues of male dominance, gender roles, and bilingualism in Latino families.

6.　be familiar with the family structure of Asian American families, the significance of generational conflict in these families, and be able to identify the myths and facts surrounding the model-minority concept.

7. understand the pervasive problems surrounding prejudice and discrimination in American society, including the contradiction between success and self-help.

8. be able to compare and contrast the Latino, American Indian, African American, and Asian-American responses to prejudice and discrimination.

9. be able to identify processes involved in raising biracial children.

10. be able to explain the reasons for the increase in interracial and interethnic marriages in the U.S. today.

CHAPTER OVERVIEW

THE INCREASING DIVERSITY OF U.S. FAMILIES

American households are becoming more diverse in terms of racial and ethnic composition. As the number and variety of immigrants increase, the ways in which we relate to each other become more complex. While some people believe that immigrants should become acculturated as soon as possible, others argue that maintaining important aspects of immigrants' original cultures strengthens and revives U.S. culture.

The United States is essentially a country of immigrants. Since the turn of the century there has been a significant shift in the numbers of immigrants coming from various countries. In 1997, Europeans made up only 17 percent of all new immigrants; today's immigrants are primarily from Asia and Latin America. Today's proportion of foreign born is small by historical standards (About 14 percent of the total U.S. population was foreign born in 1920 compared to 8 percent in 1990.). The growth of several major metropolitan areas (e.g. New York and Los Angeles) accelerated in the mid-1990s as immigrants replaced native-born Americans who left for other parts of the country. Internal migrations such as these have ignited a resurgence of nativism. The worst discrimination against immigrants tends to occur during troubled economic times when immigrants are viewed as taking jobs and disrupting economic opportunity of native-born Americans and overloading schools and welfare systems.

The most important characteristic of a minority group is its domination by a more powerful group. Race and ethnicity are two of the most important physical and cultural characteristics that single out minority groups from a dominant societal group. A group that has both distinctive racial and cultural characteristics is referred to as a racial-ethnic group. African Americans, Native Americans, Latinos, and Asian Americans are all examples of racial-ethnic groups.

AFRICAN AMERICAN FAMILIES

Prejudice, a negative attitude, and discrimination, a behavior, continue to be pervasive problems that affect all racial-ethnic families in areas like housing, employment, and education. Despite widespread beliefs that minority families are passive and dependent on welfare, research demonstrates that racial-ethnic families have resisted oppression, organized their own self-help groups, and have achieved a measure of success through political processes.

African American families are heterogeneous. They vary in terms of kinship structure, values, lifestyles, and social class. Despite such variations, many myths still surround the black family. There is an important relationship between family structure and economic well being. The text focuses on children living with one or both parents and on the impact of economic factors on family formation.

African American children have a greater likelihood of growing up with only one parent than do children in other racial-ethnic families. There are a variety of economic factors that have narrowed the pool of eligible African American men at all social class levels. Black unemployment rates are twice as high as those of whites, and the median income of black families is about half that of whites. Many young black men face very troubled futures, and those African American men who are married fare only slightly better.

A long-standing controversy has revolved around the quality of the relationships between African American males and females, both within and outside the family. Although the black middle class is expanding, it is still small. A disproportionately large number of blacks do not have college degrees, work in low-paying jobs, have higher unemployment rates, and are more likely to be poor.

There are many misconceptions about parenthood and child rearing in African American families. Although black families are stereotyped as matriarchal, the egalitarian family pattern (where both men and women share equal authority) is actually the most common authority pattern. Another misconception is that the African American father is usually absent; in fact, even fathers who are not married to the mother are often involved in parenting their children.

142

The extended family is a prevalent feature of black households. What appears to be a broken home to outsiders may be a strong extended family network. The black family may depend more on kinship ties than on marital stability. In general, the extended family is an important support network for many black Americans. Despite economic adversity, many blacks feel that their families are cohesive, they love their children, and typically teach their children to be proud of their cultural heritage. Even when resources are modest, one of the strengths of the African American family is to absorb other people into the family structure through informal adoption.

AMERICAN INDIAN FAMILIES

In 1998, American Indians made up almost one percent of the total U.S. population. American Indian families are struggling to overcome enormous economic and cultural handicaps. Native American families overcome enormous economic and cultural handicaps. Native American families are complex and diverse. Native Americans speak different languages, practice different religions and customs, and maintain different economies and political styles. Due to assimilation, there has been a massive loss of languages, customs, and values over the past decade among a number of tribes. At the same time, a strong sense of tribalism and pride in their heritage has enabled Native Americans to maintain their families.

The prevalence of traditional, couple-headed households with children is higher among Native American families than in black or white families. Extended families are still important today and are fairly common on Native American reservations. Among the most critical problems surrounding Native American families are unemployment, premarital pregnancy, and alcohol abuse. These behaviors are likely related to a loss of cultural identity and continued government and economic exploitation. In recent years, Native Americans have become increasingly aggressive in trying to solve some of the problems brought on by poverty and assimilation into white society.

LATINO FAMILIES

There is also a great deal of variation among Latino families; the many different Spanish-speaking groups in the United States vary widely. Much of the variation depends on when the groups settled in the United States, where they come from, and how they adapted to economic and political problems. Median incomes in Latino households are considerably lower than in white or Asian households and only slightly higher than in African American households.

Poor or affluent, Hispanic Americans have managed to preserve a strong family system despite discrimination and prejudice. Familism and the strength of the extended family have provided emotional and economic support to Latino people. Recent research on Latino families challenges the stereotypes introduced by earlier white and Latino investigators who saw the Latino family as rigid, cold, and unstable or as warm nurturing, and cohesive, respectively. In fact, family structure and dynamics vary greatly according to social class and the degree of assimilation.

One of the most widespread myths associated with Hispanic Americans is *machismo*; a growing body of evidence shows that this has been a grossly exaggerated misrepresentation of Hispanic-American men and conjugal relationships. On the other hand, some writers feel that *machismo* is deeply internalized in many Latino families.

ASIAN AMERICAN FAMILIES

Like Latino families, Asian American families are far from homogeneous. All families of Asian origin are continually being pressured to change old ways and adapt to American culture. Some of these changes are in family structure, socialization practices, parent-child relationships, and intergenerational interaction. Asian-American family structure varies depending on the family's origin, when the immigrants arrived, whether or not their homeland was ravaged by war, and the socioeconomic status of parents.

The major socialization values are very similar for most Asian-American families. There is an emphasis on group cooperation, filial piety, and obedience, as well as responsibility and obligation to the family. As children become more thoroughly assimilated, however, their attitudes about marriage and family life tend to become dissimilar to those of their parents.

In many Asian American families, males are valued more than females. Women are typically subordinate to men and serve as caretakers. The role of the male as the authority figure may be slowly changing, however. In many cases, working outside of the home has not decreased the Vietnamese American wife's homemaker role. Also important among some recent immigrant Vietnamese families is the expansion of women's roles beyond such traditional work as childcare and housework.

What often keeps many new immigrant families together is tradition, religion, and cultural bonds brought with them from their homeland. In some Asian American families, American-born children are rapidly outnumbering family members who were born outside the United States. How quickly children assimilate may also reflect parental assimilation. Some recent refugee families face even more serious problems with assimilation. The most traditional families have experienced the greatest intergenerational conflict. As a group, Asian American families have maintained most of their cultural identity and have remained cohesive despite assimilation and intergenerational differences.

Asian Americans are the victims of various stereotypes, but the most damaging may be the "model minority" stereotype. The notion that Asian Americans have overcome all barriers facing them obscures the real problems this group still encounters in American society. The best-publicized characteristic of Asian Americans is their exceptional performance in education, which most Americans view as the gateway to success. Many Asian-American families have become successful because those immigrants who have been admitted to the United States represent the "cream-of-the-crop" in their own country and because Asian values and traditions are very compatible with American capitalistic values for success. Many Asians arrive in the United States with few skills and low educational levels: They are young, not well educated, and often very poor. Lumping all Asians together and treating them as a model minority ignores many subgroups that are not doing well because of academic and economic difficulties.

INTERRACIAL/INTERETHNIC MARRIAGES AND RAISING BIRACIAL CHILDREN

Laws against miscegenation (marriage or sexual relations between a man and a woman of different races) existed in America as early as 1661 and weren't overturned nationally until 1967, in the U.S. Supreme Court's *Loving v. Virginia* decision. Interracial and interethnic marriages in the United States have increased slowly.

There are a number of reasons for the increase in interracial and interethnic marriages – the integration of various U.S. institutions, increased socioeconomic mobility for African Americans, acculturation of ethnic groups, a large pool of other-race eligible partners, and changing attitudes toward interracial and interethnic marriages. There is also some evidence that interracial marriage is a source of upward mobility (at least for some white women).

There is a concern about biracial children by both the white and black communities. Others, such as black social workers feel that parents who adopt biracial children are unlikely or unprepared to teach black children about their heritage.

145

Because there are no national data comparing the development of single-race and biracial children, it's impossible to know how biracial children fare. Several studies based on small and nonrandom samples, however, suggest that most biracial adolescents have positive self-concepts, high self-esteem, and about the same percentage of behavioral problems as their single-race peers.

CURRENT APPLICATIONS

1.   If you read the newspapers or watch CNN, no doubt you have learned about the resurgence of racism on our nation's college and university campuses. It seems ironic that this kind of behavior is occurring within our system of higher education, given the egalitarian emphasis that characterizes university curricula. What do you think explains this resurgence of ethnic and racial hostility? Focus your analysis on the state of the American economy and how economic hard times seem to fuel prejudice, discrimination, and stereotyping. Apparently, the Rodney King beating, the O.J. Simpson trial, and the Amadou Diallo killing have served to exacerbate people's feelings about race; some analysts feel that the Simpson affair actually *intensified* racism, for African Americans as well as for whites. What do you think?

2.   Most communities have organizations whose goal it is to protect the interests of particular ethnic or racial groups (the NAACP, the Jewish Defense League, the Mexican American Political Association, etc.). Seek out the representatives of these or other similar organizations and see if you can arrange for a meeting with them to talk about some of the issues presented in this chapter. This will not only expose you to a broad range of views concerning prejudice and discrimination, but it will also help you to understand how problems surrounding the family are grounded in the political process.

3.   It can be enlightening and even disturbing for you to confront some of your own prejudices. One way to do this is to complete the Bogardus Social Distance Scale or some equivalent. You can ask your instructor to help you locate the scale. Even if you cannot access one of the specific instruments, ask yourself whether you would want to marry a person of a different race or a different ethnic background. Provided that you would consider doing so, what problems do you anticipate in rearing a mixed-race or mixed-ethnicity child? Make a list of your thoughts.

4. Latino families receive a lot of negative publicity in the form of news stories and television specials concerning gangland activities in the barrios, the intense loyalties shared by "homeboys," and drive-by shootings. In your text, the issue is raised of how accurate the *machismo* ideology really is among Latino males. How do you perceive Latinos and Latinas? To what extent are your views predicated upon real-life experiences in dealing with Hispanic Americans versus what you have learned from the media? Do you think your impressions are totally accurate? Why or why not?

KEY TERMS FILL-IN

1. _____ is the process of adopting the language, values, beliefs, roles, or other characteristics of a host culture, in effect, it is a "blending in" process.

2. _____ refers to maintaining aspects of immigrants' original cultures while living peacefully with the host culture.

3. _____ is a concept that describes policies and practices that favor native-born citizens (as opposed to immigrants).

4. _____ is an individual's or group's cultural identity.

5. The most important characteristic of a _____ group is its domination by a more powerful group.

6. A group that has distinctive racial and cultural characteristics is referred to as a _____-_____ group.

7. _____ refers to negative attitudes about an individual or group.

8. _____ refers to behavior or actions that treat people unfairly or on the basis of their race, national origin or other characteristics.

MULTIPLE CHOICE

1. The "blending in" or adoption of the language, values, beliefs, and roles and/or other characteristics of a host culture is called:
   a. assimilation.
   b. acculturation.
   c. pluralism.
   d. exacerbation.

2. Suppose that an immigrant group maintains aspects of its original culture, but lives peacefully with the host culture. This pattern reflects:
   a. cultural pluralism.
   b. nativism.
   c. acculturation.
   d. assimilation.

3. The targets of nativism in the U.S. today are:
   a. Mexicans.
   b. Central Americans.
   c. Asians.
   d. all of the above.

4. The most important characteristic of a minority group is its:
   a. size.
   b. configuration.
   c. domination by a more powerful group.
   d. absence of prejudice.

5. _____ is a negative *attitude*.
   a. Discrimination
   b. Cultural pluralism
   c. Prejudice
   d. Genocide

6. _____ is *behavior*.
   a. Discrimination
   b. Prejudice
   c. Assimilation
   d. Cultural pluralism

7. Louis Wirth explicitly defined a _____ group in terms of its subordinate position.
    a.   majority
    b.   minority
    c.   ethnic
    d.   racial

8. Blacks, American Indians, Hispanics, and Asian Americans are examples of _____ groups.
    a.   racial-ethnic
    b.   dominant-ethnic
    c.   ethnocentric
    d.   racial-centric

9. Which of the following is/are (a) myth(s) about the African American family?
    a.   Most black families are poor and on welfare.
    b.   The black family collapsed after emancipation.
    c.   Black families no longer face widespread job and housing discrimination.
    d.   All of the above are myths.

10. According to the text's discussion of African American husbands and wives:
    a.   studies show that most black families are unhappy with their marital lives.
    b.   black husbands are more likely than their white counterparts to share in household chores.
    c.   the division of domestic work is equal.
    d.   all of the above

11. According to the text's discussion of parents and children among black families:
    a.   many black fathers make a conscious effort to be involved with their children because their own fathers were aloof.
    b.   a national study found that black parents were more likely than their white and Latino counterparts to have someone in the family teach preschoolers letters, words, numbers, and songs.
    c.   intact middle-class black families are very similar to their white counterparts in terms of parenting.
    d.   all of the above

12. In a study of low-income black families conducted by Burton, caregivers were observed to meet the needs of family members in three ways. Which of the following is NOT one of these?
    a. They helped socialize and parent the children of adolescent mothers.
    b. They provided extensive instrumental aid and emotional support to adolescent, young-adult, midlife, and elderly family members.
    c. They contributed economically by working at second jobs.
    d. They met the daily needs of family members who could not care for themselves.

13. Black unemployment rates are _____ as high as are those of whites.
    a. twice
    b. three times
    c. four times
    d. six times

14. According to the discussion of the impact of the economy on African American families:
    a. the median family incomes of African Americans are the highest of all racial-ethnic households.
    b. black unemployment rates are twice as high as those of whites.
    c. middle-class blacks who have "made it" in professional and other white-collar jobs have as many financial assets as their white counterparts.
    d. all of the above

15. Prior to the mid-1980s, much of the research on African American families emphasized the
    a. strengths of these families.
    b. problems that these families face.
    c. underclass position of African Americans.
    d. none of the above.

16. American Indians from their earliest cultures have placed a high value on:
    a. tribalism and pride in their heritage.
    b. success and independence.
    c. machismo and religion.
    d. harmony and hard work.

17. According to the text, among the Navajo and the Apache, _____ are important family members.
    a. sons
    b. cousins
    c. grandparents
    d. aunts and uncles

18. Regarding the health and economic well-being of American Indian families, the text points out that:
    a. suicide rates are high among American Indians, especially among teenagers and men under the age of 40.
    b. American Indians have lower unemployment rates than do other racial-ethnic families.
    c. poverty rates are fairly low among American Indians.
    d. all of the above.

19. According to the text's discussion of American Indians and alcohol use:
    a. most American Indian reservations permit the sale of alcohol.
    b. American Indians under age 35 are about as likely to die from diseases directly associated with alcoholism as are other U.S. residents.
    c. about 75 percent of the alcohol-related deaths among American Indians are due to sporadic, binge drinking rather than to chronic alcoholism.
    d. none of the above

20. A strength of American Indian families cited in the text is/are:
    a. relational bonding.
    b. a spirituality that sustains the family's identity and place in the world.
    c. putting community and family needs above individual achievements.
    d. all of the above.

21. Familism is often seen as a major characteristic of _____ families.
    a. Chinese
    b. African American
    c. Latino
    d. American Indian

22. The concept of *machismo* includes such elements as:
    a.   deference.
    b.   honor.
    c.   a sense of disrespect for others.
    d.   passivity.

23. Research involving Latino families suggests that:
    a.   working mothers in Puerto Rican families are primarily responsible for the care of the home and the children.
    b.   Central American men in working-class households balked at sharing household responsibilities and child care even when women worked full time outside the home.
    c.   relatively few Mexican American women have egalitarian relationships with their husbands.
    d.   all of the above

24. The text specifies four different Vietnamese family patterns in the United States. Which of the following is NOT one of these?
    a.   the nuclear family
    b.   the extended family
    c.   the one-person family
    d.   the conjugal family

25. In discussing Asian American families, the text points out that:
    a.   major socialization values are very similar for most Asian American families.
    b.   unlike American parents, Chinese parents are less likely to shield their children from family adversity.
    c.   there is some evidence that gender-role socialization is still very traditional in many Asian American families.
    d.   all of the above.

26. According to the text's discussion, which of the following is/are desirable qualities in children according to first-generation Asian Americans?
    a.   become a professional athlete
    b.   have three hobbies: studying, studying, and studying
    c.   emphasize leisure pursuits
    d.   aspire to be a recreational director

27. In a study of Asian-Indian families, the major areas of conflict between parents and children centered on:
    a. generational and cultural differences.
    b. employment.
    c. the relationship between the sexes.
    d. education.

28. Perhaps the most important catalyst in the success of Asian Americans is their exceptional performance in
    a. employment.
    b. education.
    c. business.
    d. science.

29. The 1967 U.S. Supreme Court decision that overturned miscegenation laws nationally was:
    a. *Loving v. Virginia.*
    b. *Roe v. Wade.*
    c. *Plessy v. Fegruson.*
    d. *Chilingsworth v. Sullivan.*

30. The reason(s) why interracial and interethnic marriage rates have increased in the U.S. is:
    a. acculturation.
    b. a large pool of other-race eligible partners.
    c. changing attitudes toward interracial and interethnic marriages.
    d. all of the above.

ANSWERS

KEY TERMS FILL-IN

ANSWERS	PAGE NUMBERS
1. Acculturation	305
2. Cultural pluralism	305
3. Nativism	305
4. Ethnicity	306
5. minority	306
6. racial-ethnic	306
7. Prejudice	307

MULTIPLE CHOICE

ANSWERS		PAGE NUMBERS
1.	b	305
2.	a	305
3.	d	305-306
4.	c	306
5.	c	307
6.	a	307
7.	b	306
8.	a	306
9.	d	309
10.	b	308-309
11.	d	310
12.	c	311
13.	a	312
14.	b	312
15.	b	312
16.	a	313
17.	c	315
18.	a	315
19.	c	316
20.	d	317
21.	c	319
22.	b	320
23.	d	321
24.	d	322
25.	a	322
26.	b	324
27.	a	325
28.	b	326
29.	a	328
30.	d	329

13

FAMILIES AND WORK: FACING THE ECONOMIC SQUEEZE

CHAPTER OBJECTIVES

Based upon their reading and careful consideration of Chapter Thirteen, students should:

1. be familiar with the economic health of the family in terms of economic distress, poverty, and homelessness.

2. understand the dynamics of the rich getting richer, the shrinking middle class, and the working class barely surviving.

3. be familiar with poverty in the United States, including the poverty status of children, the elderly, women, racial-ethnic families, the working poor, poverty in the suburbs, programs for poor families, and homeless families.

4. be familiar with families' efforts to adapt to changing employment trends and understand the socioeconomic implications of low-wage jobs, moonlighting, shift work, part-time jobs, overtime demands, and unemployment.

5. be familiar with the variations on traditional economic roles within marriage, including the two-person single career and the househusband.

6. understand the circumstances surrounding the combination of family and work roles, including women's increasing participation in the labor force.

7. be acquainted with dual-earner families and be able to discuss the costs and benefits of dual-career relationships, trailing spouses, and commuter marriages.

8.   understand the effect of work on family dynamics, including marital quality, spouses' welfare, and children's well-being.

9.   be familiar with the dynamics of discrimination in the workplace, including the mommy track, the daddy penalty, the gender gap in wages, and sexual harassment.

10. be acquainted with pregnancy discrimination laws, the benefits and limitations of family and medical leave policies, and types of care for children and the elderly.

11. be able to discuss the pros and cons of employees working at home.

CHAPTER OVERVIEW

MACROECONOMIC CHANGES AFFECTING THE FAMILY

Economic resources continue to play a major role in what happens to families today. Recent investigations demonstrate that a small proportion of affluent families are getting richer, but at the same time, an increasing number of middle-income families are NOT making economic progress, or are even experiencing difficulty with regard to socioeconomic issues like employment and economic deprivation. The middle class is shrinking, due to technological changes, the fact that the industrial structure of the economy has changed, the growth of two-earner families, and changes in the age composition of the population. While the rich get richer and the middle class shrinks, the working class is barely surviving, with working-class families teetering on the brink of poverty. This phenomenon is due to the fact that technological changes have replaced many manual workers with machines; the entire industrial structure of the economy has changed; the numbers of single-parent households, young workers with low salaries, and elderly women with small fixed incomes have increased; and many American corporations are exporting jobs or to third-world countries.

The *poverty line* is the minimal level of income that the federal government considers necessary for individuals' and families' basic subsistence. Authorities disagree on the validity of official poverty statistics. Some scholars feel that poverty rates are exaggerated because they have been based on figures that overstate inflation and because they ignore noncash benefits from the government, such as food stamps, housing subsidies, and medical services. Others feel that the proportion of the poor is underestimated because the amount of money needed for subsistence varies drastically by region and because many people are missed by the U.S. census counts. In any case, poverty rates are not random: Many of the poor include children, the elderly, women, and racial-ethnic minorities. There is a widespread perception that the poor are simply looking for handouts from the government, but many poor people work, and working does not guarantee staying out of poverty, and the poor are not, in fact, a bunch of loafers and parasites; almost one-fifth of all full-time workers now fall into the category of the working poor, typically defined as people or families who work full time but are barely staying above the poverty line.

Regarding programs for poor families, government policies include three types of programs: cash support, direct provisions of necessities, and compensatory or remedial education. None of these programs really helps families get off welfare. In fact, as emphasized by Herbert Gans, poverty actually has many functions.

One of the most devastating consequences of poverty is homelessness. More than half of the homeless are members of minority groups, but the homeless population in any one place reflects local and regional population trends. In 1996, the homeless estimate was at 842,000 people. An estimated 34 percent of the homeless population includes families with children. Some people attribute homelessness to "work aversion," and although this may be true of some people, such perspectives ignore changing employment trends that have had a negative impact on many families.

FAMILIES' EFFORTS TO ADAPT TO CHANGING ECONOMIC TRENDS

Across the country, families are struggling to survive. In this effort, families have adopted a variety of techniques, including taking low-paying jobs, moonlighting, working shifts, doing part-time work, and working overtime; if and when these tactics fail, they join the ranks of the unemployed. Families living under the threat of unemployment experience problems in communication and in problem solving, and relationships among spouses and children suffer. Another reason for unemployment is the phenomenon of the discouraged worker. Many experts feel that unemployment rates are misleading because they ignore the underemployed worker.

NEW ECONOMIC ROLES WITHIN MARRIAGE

Because of economic changes, a traditional marital role in which the man is the provider and the woman is the homemaker has been decreasing. Although they are not widespread, there are two variations on traditional marriage roles: The two-person single career and the househusband. Many breadwinners and homemakers enjoy the traditional family structure, but there are costs to each.

JUGGLING FAMILY AND WORK ROLES

Not all women accept the traditional homemaker role as their role model. Many adolescents and college students say that they expect to combine both work and family. They feel that work is not a top priority but also expect to have a house, several cars, state-of-the-art recreational equipment, and other amenities. Furthermore, more young men than young women expect the wife to stay home with the children instead of seeking a career. Thus, the expectations of many young people may be unrealistic and contradictory. There are two major reasons for the increase in the numbers of working women: individual fulfillment and supporting themselves and their dependents.

DUAL-EARNER FAMILIES

Economic recessions have resulted in more dual-earner families. There is a great deal of variation in this category of family: dual-career marriages, trailing spouses, commuter marriages, and marriages in which wives earn more than their husbands. Dual-earner couples are married partners both of whom are employed outside the home. Such couples are also referred to as dual-income, two-earner, or dual-worker couples. Dual-career couples are marriage partners both of whom work in professional or managerial positions. Trailing spouses refers to partners who give up their work and search for another position in the location where a spouse has taken a job. In a commuter marriage, married partners live and work in different geographic areas and get together intermittently. The major dilemma for commuter couples is role transition, but an equally difficult problem is the supersuccess syndrome. The few available studies of wives who earn more than their husbands suggest that these relationships often become troubled or disintegrate. Employment, whether in two-paycheck families, dual-career marriages, or commuter marriages, affects the family in many ways. Whether the results are positive or negative, work roles influence the duration and quality of a marriage, household labor, and children" well-being. "Family work" refers to household chores and child-care tasks that must be performed by families to maintain the household and its members.

INEQUALITY IN THE WORKPLACE

Employed women are frequently romanticized. In reality, and regardless of the occupation, most women face similar problems in terms of sex-segregated workplaces (the "mommy track" and the "daddy penalty"), wage discrimination (comparable worth), and sexual harassment. The "mommy track" refers to career-and-family women who combine career with child rearing. In what appears to be a backhanded attempt to keep women out of the workplace, some corporations are apparently penalizing the husbands of women who work outside the home, a phenomenon that has been called the "daddy penalty." According to many different studies, gender still explains the earnings differential between women and men. Comparable worth is a concept that calls for equal pay for both males and females doing work that requires comparable skill, effort, and responsibility, and is performed under similar working conditions. Sexual harassment can take many forms and takes place throughout the world; it can be very costly to everyone involved. Many companies have instituted grievance procedures for victims of sexual harassment.

IS THE WORKPLACE FAMILY FRIENDLY?

The workplace may appear not to be very family friendly, but pregnancy discrimination laws now give considerable protection to pregnant workers and their jobs, and family leave policies have made it easier to care for newborns and ill family members. On the other hand, provisions for childcare and elder care still leave a great deal to be desired. One of the most serious problems facing families today is inadequate day care for young children. Elder-care services are rarely provided or even subsidized by business as yet, but some companies are now providing employee seminars on a variety of elder-care topics. While combining family and work is not impossible, there is a negative side to the trend.

CURRENT APPLICATIONS

1. The text points out that in terms of the economic health of the family, the rich are getting richer, the middle class is shrinking, and the working class is barely surviving. Based upon your own socioeconomic position, how do you react to this forecast? If you plan to have children or are already a parent, how do you feel this phenomenon will affect your sons' and/or daughters' future(s)? Do you foresee any social event(s) that might alter the course of these trends? Why or why not?

2. Some critics have responded to the controversy over homemaker-breadwinner roles (specifically that women should be able to have careers and not be expected to be full-time homemakers) by insisting that someone, whether the persona is female or male,

159

should serve in the capacity of homemaker, for the overall well being of families. These observers argue that it is important for one member of a family to be responsible for "taking care of the home base." In the discussion of "househusbands" in the text, it is pointed out that few men nationwide have assumed this role on a full-time basis. What do you think about the argument that *someone* should assume the role of "homemaker"? Make a list of the pros and cons to this argument. Discuss the issues with other members of your class.

3. Do you think that commuter marriages are viable? Is it really true that the "family that plays together stays together"? Are commuter marriages for everyone? Do you think that you could have a successful commuter marriage? Why or why not?

4. Most colleges and universities now have a specific *sexual harassment policy.* In your experience as a student, do you feel that you have been the victim of sexual harassment? If not, have you spoken to anyone who has, or do you think that you have witnessed an incident of this type of behavior? What, in your judgment, constitutes sexual harassment? The text presents a few examples of distinctions between acceptable behavior and sexual harassment. Where do you feel that acceptable behavior leaves off and sexual harassment begins? Make a list of examples of your own and discuss these with other members of your class.

KEY TERMS FILL-IN

1. The _____ _____ is the minimal level of income that the federal government considers necessary for individuals' and families' basic needs.

2. The index of prices that measures the change in the cost of prices that measures the cost of basic goods and services in comparison to a fixed base period is called the _____ _____ index.

3. Researcher Diana Pearce (1978) referred to the increased likelihood that female heads of households will be poor as the _____ of poverty.

4. People who work full-time but are barely staying above the poverty line are categorized as the _____-poor.

5. The _____ _____ wants a job and has looked for work during the preceding year but has not searched in the month prior to a survey because of the belief that job-hunting efforts are futile.

6. The phenomenon of the _____ worker includes those who have part-time jobs but would rather be working full-time as well as those who accept jobs below their skill and educational levels.

7. In the _____-_____ _____ career variation, one spouse typically the wife, participates in the partner's career behind the scenes without pay or direct recognition.

8. _____ are those rare men who stay home to care for the family and do the housework while their wives are the wage earners.

9. A _____-_____ couple refers to spouses who work in occupations that are defined as other than professional or managerial.

10. _____ income is income that people can spend as they please after paying for basic necessities.

11. A _____-_____ couple refers to marriage partners who both work in professional or managerial positions that require extensive training, a long-term commitment, and offer ongoing professional growth.

12. The _____ _____ is the spouse who gives up his or her job and searches for another position in a new location because the partner has been relocated or obtained new employment.

13. A _____ marriage involves spouses who live and work in different geographical areas and get together intermittently.

14. Women who are employed part-time and able to spend more time at home (career-and-family women) are frequently referred to in the media as being on a _____ _____.

MULTIPLE CHOICE

1.   In 1979, the average family income in the top 5 percent of the earnings distribution was more than ten times that of the bottom 20 percent. By 1999, this ratio had increased by _____ to 1.
      a.   16
      b.   17
      c.   18
      d.   19

2.   The text suggests that the middle class has been shrinking for a number of reasons, including:
      a.   the prosperity gap has increased because many people work in the "old economy" versus the "new economy."
      b.   the income gains from the new economy have gone, disproportionately, to those with high incomes.
      c.   only the most highly skilled workers are prospering in the new economy.
      d.   all of the above

3.   The reason(s) cited in the text for the dire financial predicament of working-class families is/are:
      a.   technological changes have replaced many manual workers with machines.
      b.   the entire industrial structure of the economy has changed.
      c.   many U.S. corporations have been exporting white-collar and blue-collar jobs overseas or to third-world countries.
      d.   all of the above are reasons cited in the text.

4.   The minimal level of income that the federal government considers necessary for individuals' and families' subsistence is referred to as the:
      a.   marketbasket index.
      b.   poverty line.
      c.   relative poverty index.
      d.   basic standard of living.

5.   In 1999, the poverty line for a family of four was:
      a. $12,420.
      b. $17,029.
      c. $19,240
      d. $21,690.

6. The major reason(s) cited in the text for the feminization of poverty is/are:
   a. wage discrimination.
   b. job discrimination.
   c. divorce.
   d. all of the above are reasons cited in the text.

7. According to Gans (1971), ensuring that the dirty work gets done, subsidizing the middle and upper classes by working for low wages, and purchasing of goods and services that would otherwise be rejected, are some of the functions of:
   a. poverty.
   b. welfare.
   c. tax incentives.
   d. ADC.

8. Which of the following is NOT one of the functions of poverty and inequality as specified by sociologist Herbert Gans?
   a. They ensure that society's work gets done.
   b. The poor subsidize the middle and upper classes by working for low wages.
   c. The poor are built-in "deviants."
   d. The poor absorb the costs of societal change and community growth.

9. _____ workers want a job and have looked for work during the preceding year, but have not searched recently because they believe that their efforts are futile.
   a. Discouraged
   b. Displaced
   c. Two-person, single career
   d. Underemployed

10. Workers who have part-time jobs but would rather be working full-time, as well as those who accept jobs below their level of job experience are referred to as _____.
    a. discouraged
    b. underemployed
    c. marginally employed
    d. part-time

11. The text cites Moen's four categories of working mothers. Which of the following is NOT one of these categories?
   a. captives
   b. copers
   c. the conflicted
   d. the coopted

12. The most important predictor of who the trailing spouse will be is:
   a. income.
   b. one's sex.
   c. how many children are in the family.
   d. the state of the economy.

13. A common problem faced by partners in commuter marriages is/are:
   a. role transition.
   b. the supersuccess syndrome.
   c. physical exhaustion.
   d. all of the above.

14. Which of the following is true of commuter marriages?
   a. The major motivation of commuter couples is financial security.
   b. Even couples with young children find commuting is worth the stress they experience.
   c. Most commuting partners work a maximum of only 8-10 hour days during the week
   d. Partners in such marriages typically see their work as an integral part of their self-concept.

15. The division of family work varies by:
   a. social class.
   b. occupational level.
   c. racial and national origin.
   d. all of the above.

16. In dual-earner families, the determining factor of how a mother's employment impacts on the child's development is:
   a. how many hours the mother works each week.
   b. the ability of the husband to assume the role of "nurturer."
   c. the quality of child care—parental or nonparental—available.
   d. all of the above are equally important.

17. Sexual harassment was first designated an illegal form of sex discrimination in:
    a. 1954.
    b. 1964.
    c. 1974
    d. 1984.

18. Which of the following is NOT an illustration of sexual harassment?
    a. A male supervisor tells a female employee that "You look very nice today."
    b. An employee continues to ask someone for dates despite the person's repeated refusals.
    c. Employees or supervisors make frequent comments to co-workers on sexually printed material in the media.
    d. A male employee frequently brushes up against female employees "accidentally."

19. Under the Family and Medical Leave Act:
    a. any employee is eligible who has worked at least 1250 hours during a 12-month period.
    b. an employee may take family or medical leave for the birth or adoption of a child and to care for a newborn; to care for a spouse, child, or parent with a serious illness; and to recuperate from a serious illness that prevents an employee from working.
    c. the employee pays for the leave.
    d. all of the above

20. According to the text, feminists have argued that the _____ concept gave employers reasons not to hire or promote talented women to high-level positions and that it perpetuated gender-role stereotypes.
    a. displaced homemaker
    b. discretionary track
    c. mommy track
    d. two-person single career

21. In what some see as a backhanded attempt to keep women out of the workplace, some corporations are apparently paying husbands whose wives work outside of the home *less* than their counterparts in traditional families where wives are full-time homemakers. This phenomenon has been referred to as the:
   a. daddy penalty.
   b. father liability.
   c. daddy trap.
   d. househusband track.

22. One of the most important pieces of legislation for many families is the _____ Act, which was first introduced into Congress in 1985 and finally signed into law by President Clinton in 1993.
   a. Pregnancy Discrimination
   b. Family and Medical Leave
   c. Dependent Day Care
   d. Working-Women

23. *Telecommuting* refers to:
   a. a commuter marriage.
   b. working from home through computer hookups to a company office.
   c. commuting to and from work via high-speed public transportation.
   d. commuting to work using air travel.

24. The Family and Medical Leave Act (FMLA)'s biggest limitation is that:
   a. all leave must be taken at one time.
   b. U.S. employees who work in companies with fewer than 50 employees aren't covered by the Act.
   c. employers are required to save the job for anyone taking a leave, even when it causes substantial economic injury.
   d. all of the above are weaknesses of the act.

ANSWERS

KEY TERMS FILL-IN

ANSWERS	**PAGE NUMBERS**
1. poverty line	337

MULTIPLE CHOICE

ANSWERS   **PAGE NUMBERS**

14

FAMILY VIOLENCE AND OTHER CRISIS-RELATED ISSUES

CHAPTER OBJECTIVES

Based upon their reading and careful consideration of Chapter Fourteen, students should:

1. understand the implications of marital and intimate partner violence.

2. be familiar with the characteristics of the violent household.

3. be able to identify and discuss the three phases of the cycle of domestic violence.

4. be familiar with the circumstances surrounding marital rape.

5. understand the reasons why women remain in abusive situations.

6. be acquainted with the issues surrounding the abuse of men by women.

7. be familiar with the definition, rates, and causes of child abuse, and be able to discuss the characteristics of victims and assailants in terms of race, ethnicity, and social class.

8. be able to identify the characteristics of the incestuous home, be familiar with the implications of sexual abuse, and the impact of violence on children.

9. understand why siblings and elderly people may be "hidden victims" of family violence and abuse.

10. be familiar with the theories of family violence: patriarchy/male-dominance, social learning, resource, conflict, and exchange.

11. be able to discuss the benefits and barriers to prevention and treatment programs.

12. understand how drugs, depression, anorexia, bulimia, and steroids affect the health of adolescents and other family members.

13. be familiar with the impact of the death of a child on the family.

14. be familiar with the right-to-die controversy.

CHAPTER OVERVIEW

Families can be warm, loving, and nurturing, but they can also be cruel and abusive. People are more likely to be killed or assaulted by family members than by outsiders. Gelles (1997) observes, "That violence and love can coexist in a household is perhaps the most insidious aspect of family violence, because we grow up learning that it is acceptable to hit the people we love."

MARITAL VIOLENCE AND INTIMATE PARTNER VIOLENCE

Marital violence and intimate partner violence may be physical or emotional. It is difficult to measure marital violence. More women are injured by their intimate partners' battering than by rapes, auto accidents, and muggings combined. Women can also be abusive, but when women are violent, they are more likely to be defending themselves than to be initiating violence and they are more likely to sustain serious physical injuries. Contrary to common wisdom, family violence does not occur only in lower socioeconomic families but cuts across racial, ethnic, religious, and social class lines. Middle-class family violence is less visible. Abusive men have been described as feeling helpless, powerless, and inadequate in both their marriages and their jobs.

The "cycle theory of battering incidents" (Walker) proposes that there is a three-phase cycle involved in marital abuse, beginning with the tension-building phase, leading to the acute battering incident, and ending with the calm that follows the incident; this cycle repeats itself over and over again.

In 1991, England passed a law that made marital rape, or wife rape, a criminal act. In the United States, approximately half of the states still do not consider raping a wife a crime. This legal right of wife rape is known as a *marital-rape exemption* (that is, they do not prosecute a rape case if the man is actually living with the woman, married or not).

According to national surveys of family violence, a clear majority of abused women seek help, but some women do not try to leave an abusive relationship. The text suggests that there are several factors that help to explain why women do not leave abusive relationships: (1) negative self-concept and low self-esteem, (2) a belief that the abuser will change, (3) economic hardship and homelessness, (4) the need for child support, (5) fear of surviving alone in a hostile world, (6) shame, guilt, and sin, (7) fear of the husband, and (8) the home becomes a prison. There are women who abuse men and husband abuse may be the most underreported form of marital violence. Three reasons why men do not protect themselves in these kinds of situations are that many men believe that only a bully would hit a woman; others fear they might hurt their wives if they fought back; while other husbands feel they could punish their wives by showing them the injuries they had inflicted and making the wives feel guilty.

VIOLENCE AGAINST CHILDREN

Child abuse is not a recent phenomenon. Child abuse is the physical or mental injury, sexual abuse, negligent treatment, or maltreatment of a child under the age of 18 by a person who is responsible for the child's welfare under circumstances that indicate that the child's health or welfare is harmed or threatened thereby. Child maltreatment is characterized by a broad range of behaviors that place the child at serious risk, subsuming physical abuse, sexual abuse, neglect, and emotional maltreatment. Estimates of the incidence of child abuse vary because of different data-collection procedures. The maltreatment of children may lead to murder. A number of problems contribute to child maltreatment, with the biggest being parental substance abuse. Other factors are the child's age and sex, the family's economic situation, the parents' marital status, and spousal abuse.

With a few exceptions, incest is forbidden in all known societies, but despite these taboos, it has been estimated that 17 percent of all Americans have been involved in an incestuous relationship. Although there is no typical incest abuser, studies have found some common characteristics, including low self-esteem, families of orientation where a repressive attitude toward sex prevailed, and receipt of little sex information from their parents. Incest is especially common in reconstituted families. Theories about the role of the mother in the incestuous family can be classified into three categories: as colluder, as helpless dependent, and as victim. Abusive behavior at home has been found to be a major cause of adolescents running away from home. Whether the abuse is sexual or not, many studies have found that abused children suffer from a variety of physiological, social, and emotional problems, including difficulty communicating, increased aggression, learning disabilities, headaches, bed wetting, chronic constipation, sleeping disorders, and poor performance in school.

HIDDEN VICTIMS: SIBLINGS AND THE ELDERLY

Violence toward spouses and children is not the only forms of domestic abuse. Less visible abuse includes violence between siblings and abuse of elderly family members. There are various forms of sibling abuse, including name-calling and ridicule, degradation, promoting fear, torturing or killing a pet, and destroying personal possessions. Some research indicates that incest and other sexual abuse are common among brothers and sisters, but this type of behavior is rarely reported. The elderly often tolerate abuse from family caretakers because they love the abusers, because they see no viable alternatives, because they are lonely, because they are afraid of depriving their grandchildren or of being deprived of contact with them, or because they have decided (unconsciously) to exchange submissiveness and passivity for the care they need. There are also cultural variations that help explain why older people tolerate abuse or neglect.

Other hidden forms of family violence that are discussed include adolescents and abuse in gay and lesbian households. Gelles' research in adolescent victims indicates that when adolescents fail to live up to their parents' expectations, parents sometimes use physical force to assert their parental control. Some teenagers strike back, both physically and verbally. In gay and lesbian households, researchers estimate that the incidence of battering between couples is about the same as it is for heterosexual couples and much of the abuse is recurrent.

Reasons for the abuse of older people include: impairment of the caregiver, impairment of the care recipient, dependency in the older person, and medial costs.

EXPLAINING FAMILY VIOLENCE

Several theories have been proposed to explain why family violence exists and, more specifically, why female vicitmization is condoned. The most pertinent explanations are patriarchy/male-dominance theory, social-learning theory, resource theory, conflict theory, and exchange theory. Patriarchy/male-dominance theory emphasizes the tendency in patriarchal societies for women and children to be defined as the property of men. Men who see women and children as property feel they are entitled to sexual access through incest or marital rape. Social-learning theory posits that aggression and violence are learned by direct experience and by observing the behavior of others. Resource theory assumes that the more social, personal, and economic resources people have, the more power they command. Conflict theorists argue that women and children are victimized in the family not only because they have few individual resources but because societal institutions rarely take violence against women and children seriously. According to exchange theory, the assailant's violent behavior carries more benefits than costs. One popular hypothesis is that violence is learned through modeling and transmitted across generations, but the evidence for this theory is mixed. So far, no one really knows whether, or how much, family violence is transmitted intergenerationally.

INTERVENING IN FAMILY VIOLENCE

Effective treatment and prevention programs will not be developed until professionals and the public acknowledge that family violence is a serious problem. Many experts in the field feel that families need help to prevent abuse before it starts. A persistent problem is the tendency to blame the victim, particularly in cases of marital abuse. Many cases of domestic violence do not come to the attention of protective-service agencies. The *battered-woman syndrome* is defined as a condition reached by a woman who has experienced many years of physical abuse and who feels incapable of leaving; in a desperate effort to defend themselves, these women sometimes kill their abusers.

OTHER CRISES IN FAMILY LIFE

In addition to violence, families must grapple with other health-related issues such as drug abuse and steroids, depression and suicide, anorexia and bulimia. The most recent issues confronting families include how to cope with the death of children.

CURRENT APPLICATIONS

1.   Seek out a police officer, a social worker who deals with domestic violence, or a counselor at a spouse abuse shelter in your college community. Make an appointment to see this person in order to talk about Walker's three-phase cycle of domestic violence (tension-building, acute battering, and calm following the battering incident). Ask this person to comment on his/her experiences with the cycle of violence "in action."

2.   In England, around the time that the colonies were preparing for the American Revolution, British law specified that it was *impossible* for a husband to rape his wife. In 1991, England passed a law that made marital rape a criminal act. In the United

States, some states grant a *marital-rape exemption* which means there is no prosecution provided that the man is living with the woman, married or not. What is going on here? Think about why the prevailing attitude has been that rape cannot take place in marriage or in a permanent relationship. Hint: Consider how women have been viewed historically as a form of property.

3. Most men and women who have great affection for children have a very difficult time understanding how anyone could be abusive toward a child. Try to imagine for yourself the kinds of conditions that are discussed in the text which cause child abuse: parental substance abuse, economic stress and poverty, wife abuse, parental conflict and family stress. Sexual abuse is likely to conjure up even more emotional feelings: How could someone sexually abuse a child? Again, engage in some role playing with respect to the kinds of conditions that contribute to sexual abuse in families: low self-esteem, a lack of self-control, a lack of information about sex, enabling by mothers, etc.

4. How do you think you would handle the situation if the care and keeping of your parents became *your responsibility*—say, for example, they became so ill that they could not care for themselves and you didn't want to send them to a nursing home? Do you think you could become so frustrated that you would abuse your parents, either physically or emotionally? This is a tough question and the tendency is surely to answer an emphatic "No." Still, by thinking about this issue in critical terms, you may be in a position to better understand the text's discussion of elder abuse.

5. A theme that is very prominent in the substance abuse field is that various additions (drugs, alcohol, eating disorders, etc.) are "diseases" that victimize people and that can be cured by the intervention of professionals such as psychologists, social workers, and substance abuse counselors. The sociologist immediately recognizes the possibility that the "disease" model is an ideology that protects and justifies the dominant role of these professionals in dealing with addictive behavior. This is a very controversial issue, but it may be helpful to confront it directly in conversation with other students and/or your peers. You may also wish to take a look at a book entitled *Heavy Drinking: The Myth of Alcoholism as a Disease*, by Herbert Fingarette (Berkeley: University of California Press, 1988). This book has generated howls of protest among substance abuse professionals, and if you know someone personally who would likely oppose Fingarette's thesis, you may wish to discuss the issues involved with him/her in order to gain additional perspective.

KEY TERMS FILL-IN

1. In 1991, England passed a law that made _____ _____ a criminal act.

2. _____ _____ is defined as the physical or mental injury, sexual abuse, negligent treatment, or maltreatment of a child under the age of 18 by a person who is responsible for the child's welfare.

3. _____ _____ is characterized by a broad range of behaviors that place the child at serious risk.

4. With few exceptions, _____ is forbidden in all known societies.

5. _____ _____ is often used as a shorthand term that encompasses physical abuse, neglect, financial exploitation, psychological abuse, and the medical abuse or neglect of people 65 or older.

6. Baby boomers are often referred to as the _____ _____ because they care not only for their own children but for their aging parents as well.

7. The _____-_____ _____ refers to women who have experienced many years of physical assaults and feel incapable of leaving.

8. _____ _____ is an eating disorder characterized by an intense fear of becoming obese coupled with a distorted body image.

9. _____ is an eating disorder characterized by a cyclical behavior of eating binges followed by self-induced vomiting, fasting, excessive exercise or the use of laxatives.

10. _____ are most often synthetic versions of testosterone.

MULTIPLE CHOICE

1. Which of the following is NOT one of the risk factors associated with family violence?
   a. The husband or male partner is sadistic, aggressive, or obsessively jealous.
   b. The family is surrounded by relatives, neighbors, and the community.
   c. The total family income is below the poverty line.
   d. The husband is under the age of 30.

2. Which of the following is NOT one of the phases of the cycle of domestic violence as proposed by Walker?
   a. the tension-building phase
   b. the acute battering incident
   c. calm
   d. the homicide stage

3. In some states, if a man is actually living with the woman who charges him with rape, whether they are married or not, the man will not be prosecuted. This loophole is referred to in the text as:
   a. a marital-rape exemption.
   b. rapist protection legislation.
   c. the wifely duty statue.
   d. the "kept woman" policy.

4. _____ is an act of violence in which a man forces his nonconsenting wife to engage in sexual intercourse.
   a. Marital rape
   b. Spousal rape
   c. Wife rape
   d. all of the above

5. The text points out that an estimated _____ percent of married women are raped by their spouses.
   a. 15
   b. 25
   c. 30
   d. 38

6. Some researchers regard _____ abuse is the most under-reported of form of family violence.
   a. husband
   b. wife
   c. elder
   d. child

7. Which of the following is NOT one of the explanations cited in the text for a victim's decision to stay with an abusive partner?
   a. a belief that the abuser will change
   b. the need for child support
   c. the lack of an adequate education
   d. the home becomes a prison

8. Three reasons have been suggested for why men often do not protect themselves when they are abused by women. Which of the following is NOT one of these?
   a. chivalry ("only a bully would hit a woman")
   b. inadequacy
   c. self-restraint
   d. punishment

9. According to the text, the biggest problem contributing to child maltreatment is:
   a. parental substance abuse.
   b. poverty.
   c. associated wife abuse.
   d. underemployment.

10. _____ includes making a child watch sexual acts, fondling of sexual organs, incest, or intercourse.
    a. Sexual abuse
    b. Emotional abuse
    c. Physical neglect
    d. Physical abuse

11. _____ includes the failure to provide for basic caretaking obligations.
    a. Sexual abuse
    b. Emotional abuse
    c. Child neglect
    d. Physical abuse

12. _____ includes such acts as belittlement, verbal abuse, and terrorizing a child by threats of physical harm.
    a. Sexual abuse
    b. Emotional maltreatment
    c. Physical neglect
    d. Physical abuse

13. Which of the following is NOT a myth concerning incest?
    a. Children lie about incest.
    b. If the child is not coerced, it is not incest.
    c. Incest happens only in poor, disorganized, and unstable families.
    d. Incest is infrequently punished by incarceration.

14. Which of the following is NOT one of the categories specified by Jacobs in his typology of mothers in incestuous families?
    a. the mother as colluder
    b. the mother as molester
    c. the mother as dependent
    d. the mother as victim

15. Which of the following is NOT one of the forms of sibling abuse as identified by Wiehe and Herring?
    a. name-calling and ridicule
    b. degradation
    c. promoting fear
    d. All of the above are forms of sibling abuse.

16. Which of the following is/are (a) recognized sign(s) of child abuse?
    a. unexplained injuries and self-destructive acts
    b. torn, stained, or bloody underclothing and excessive seductiveness
    c. speech disorders and neurotic traits
    d. all of the above.

17. According to the text, child abuse may also lead to a higher likelihood of:
    a. suicide.
    b. homosexuality.
    c. sexual immaturity.
    d. arrest for delinquency.

18. Which of the following is NOT one of the forms of sibling abuse identified in the text?
    a. name-calling and ridicule
    b. degradation
    c. telling obscene jokes
    d. destroying personal possessions

19. The text points out that elder abuse encompasses:
    a. physical abuse.
    b. negligence.
    c. financial exploitation.
    d. all of the above

20. Most studies have found that although elder abuse occurs in all age groups, the likeliest victims are middle to lower class white women between _____ years of age.
    a. 62 and 65
    b. 68 and 70
    c. 70 and 75
    d. 75 and 85

21. Persons who use steroids are likely to experience _____ as a side effect.
    a. a decrease in testosterone production
    b. disinterest in sex
    c. increased facial and body hair
    d. All of the above are possible side effects.

22. An individual suffering from _____, has extreme weight loss, an intense fear of becoming obese, and a distorted body image.
    a. bulimia
    b. obesity
    c. chronic underweight syndrome
    d. anorexia nervosa

23. Knapp (1987) found that the death of a child often results in grief that is never totally resolved. He called this grief:
    a. shadow grief.
    b. pedophilic grief.
    c. the Knapp Syndrome.
    d. latent grief.

ANSWERS

KEY TERMS FILL-IN

ANSWERS	PAGE NUMBERS
1. marital rape	370

MULTIPLE CHOICE

ANSWERS		PAGE NUMBERS
1.	b	Table 14.1 (Page 368)
2.	d	369-370
3.	a	370
4.	d	370
5.	a	370
6.	a	373
7.	c	370-372
8.	b	373
9.	a	376
10.	a	374
11.	c	374
12.	b	374
13.	d	378
14.	b	377-378
15.	d	379-380
16.	d	Table 14.3 (Page 380)
17.	d	379
18.	c	379-380
19.	d	381
20.	d	382
21.	d	390
22.	d	391
23.	a	392-393

SEPARATION AND DIVORCE

15

CHAPTER OBJECTIVES

Based upon their reading and careful consideration of Chapter Fifteen, students should:

1. be able to identify the three phases of separation and to discuss the various outcomes of marital separation.

2. understand the characteristics of divorce in terms of differences by age and gender and in reference to the process of divorce.

3. be aware that divorce is a transitional process and be familiar with Bohannon's six "stations" of divorce: emotional, legal, economic, co-parental, community, and psychic.

4. be familiar with the macro-level, demographic, and interpersonal reasons for divorce.

5. be prepared to discuss the consequences of divorce in terms of emotional and psychological effects, economic and financial changes, property settlements and alimony, child support, and custody issues.

6. be familiar with the impact that divorce has on children, including the impact of absent fathers, age- and gender-related problems, and behavioral and emotional consequences.

7. be able to identify the positive outcomes of divorce.

8. be familiar with the role of counseling and divorce mediation in making divorce a less adversarial experience.

CHAPTER OVERVIEW

Divorce rates have increased, but so have the rates of remarriage and redivorce. This means that family structures and relationships are more complex today than they were in the past. This chapter focuses on the fact that whether these changes produce costs, benefits, or both,

180

separation and divorce usually involve long-term processes and consequences.

SEPARATION: PROCESS AND OUTCOME

Separation can be temporary or permanent, and it can precede divorce, but not necessarily. In most cases, separation is a lengthy process involving four phases: preseparation, early separation, midseparation, and late separation. During *preseparation*, the couple physically separates after a gradual, emotional alienation of feelings; the *early separation* phase is beset with problems because our society does not have clear-cut rules for separating; in the *midseparation* phase, the harsh realities of everyday living set in; and during the *late separation* phase, the partners must learn how to survive as singles again.

Not all separations end in divorce. Many low-income couples experience long-term separations without divorce because they may be unable to pay the necessary legal fees; higher family income, on the other hand, typically increases the likelihood of divorce.

Approximately 10 percent of all currently married couples have separated and reconciled. Wineburg (1996) found that a successful reconciliation varies by age at separation and whether or not the woman gave birth before marrying. Women separating after age 23 were substantially more likely to reconcile than their younger counterparts. Wineberg attributes this difference to older women being more mature, more willing to reconcile because they have invested more in the marriage than their younger counterparts. If there are children, both spouses may attempt reconciliation because they have a greater commitment to marriage as an institution and often exhaust all options to save the marriage. While some couples reconcile, most separations end in divorce.

THE PROCESS OF DIVORCE

Divorce rates in the United States began a dramatic and steady climb. Since 1980, divorce rates have plateaued and dropped slightly between 1995 and 1999.

Divorces often reflect a long-term process consisting of different phases. Bohannon (1971) found that in most divorces, the participants experience a series of stages: the *emotional* divorce begins before any legal steps are taken; the *legal* divorce is the formal dissolution of the marriage (during this stage, alimony and child support are key issues); during the *economic* divorce, the partners may experience differences of opinion concerning money and property; the *coparental* divorce involves the agreements between the mother and the father about who has various responsibilities for the children; partners then go through a *community* divorce, wherein relationships with others (relatives, friends, etc.) change; finally, the couple goes through a *psychic* divorce, where the partners separate from each other emotionally. Not all couples go through all six of Bohannon's stages. Also, some couples may experience several of the stages (e.g. emotional and economic divorce) simultaneously.

WHY DO PEOPLE DIVORCE?

The increase in divorce rates can be explained on three levels: macro reasons, demographic variables, and interpersonal factors. There are many macro-level reasons, focusing on four important sources of change: social institutions, social integration, gender roles, and cultural values. There are also many demographic factors, including parental divorce, presence of children, age at marriage, premarital childbearing, race and ethnicity, education and income. Interpersonally, there are many reasons for divorce, but "falling out of love" is not the major reason for divorce. In a national study, Patterson and Kim (1992) found communication problems to be the main reason.

Divorce has a major impact in several areas: emotional and psychological problems, economic and financial changes, property settlements and psychological problems, economic and financial changes, property settlements and psychological problems, economic and financial changes, property settlements and alimony, child support (see NUTA's explanation why fathers fail to pay child support on page 438) and custody issues. In contrast to popular opinion, very few women receive substantial alimony. In addition, because child support payment is rare or the amount awarded is low, many women and children enter poverty after divorce. Nearly 50 percent of all men neither see nor support their children after a divorce. Across all races, children in two-parent households are better off financially than are those in one-parent families.

In 72 percent of the cases, the mother gets custody of the children. There are three types of custody: In sole custody, one parent has sole responsibility for raising the child; in split custody, the children are divided between the parents; and in joint custody, the children divide their time between both parents. There are two types of joint custody: *joint legal* (all major decisions concerning the children will be shared by the ex-spouses) and *joint physical* (the children actually spend a certain amount of time living with each parent). Joint custody is a controversial issue, with its fair share of opponents as well as proponents; in general, this arrangement works best when both parents want it.

HOW DOES DIVORCE AFFECT CHILDREN?

Most research has shown that divorce has detrimental effects on children, but more recently, investigators have suggested that some of the problems may exist before the divorce or may be attributed to the absence of fathers. Experts agree that first and foremost, any decisions regarding children involved in divorce should be made by keeping what is best for the child in mind. One of the most important influences on children's reactions to their parents' divorce is the parents' behavior and the way they choose to handle the situation. Recently, researchers have suggested that some problems may have existed before the divorce and that others may be attributed to the absence of one parent, usually the father.

SOME POSITIVE OUTCOMES OF DIVORCE

The major positive outcome of divorce is that it provides options to people in unsatisfactory marriages. Not surprisingly, adult children of divorce have less idealized views of marriage than do people who come from intact families. Some social scientists suggest that children who grow up in father-absence homes may be less pressured to conform to traditional gender roles and may instead learn more androgynous roles that will help them be better parents in adulthood. Gold (1992) and other clinicians have suggested that the positive aspects of divorce can be increased if adults remember to act like adults.

COUNSELING AND DIVORCE MEDIATION

Divorce mediation has emerged as an alternative to the traditional adversarial approach in the legal process. It is less bitter and less protracted and may result in both partners having a greater voice in child-custody issues. Some clinicians describe mediation as a win-win situation.

CURRENT APPLICATIONS

1. Social critics have suggested that the divorce rate would be much lower if people would more carefully consider their decisions to marry in the first place. Consider what life would be like and what changes would occur if divorce were made illegal or severely restricted? How would such a move affect people? How do you think it would influence people's decision to marry? Construct a hypothetical society along these lines.

2.	When no-fault divorce was first introduced in state legal systems, observers were optimistic that this statute would ameliorate the vagaries of the adversary approach to divorce. Now, after two decades of experience with "no-fault," it is clear that there are many problems associated with the procedure, most notably in terms of single-parent families headed by women who are receiving inadequate or no child support from the father of their children. The text discusses legal strategies that have been employed in an effort to correct this problem. What do YOU think our society could do to improve the circumstances surrounding women receiving court ordered child support payments? Construct a sketch of the strategies you would recommend.

3.	The text mentions *divorce mediation* as an alternative to traditional approaches to divorce. When couples elect divorce mediation, they mutually agree to certain arrangements, such as the specific nature of child custody or the amount of child support to be paid by one of the spouses. This is very different from having a judge point a finger at one or both parties and command that he/she/they will do certain things under penalty of law. How do you think that divorce mediation would be helpful in avoiding some of the negative impact of divorce—especially as far as the children are involved? Make a list of the advantages that you come up with.

4.	On page 408 of the text, the *Ask Yourself* insert poses the question, "Do you know someone with divorce hangover?" Make a special point to respond thoughtfully to each of the hypothetical scenarios, plugging in the name of someone you know who has recently divorced. If YOU have recently divorced, you can use yourself as the example. Or, if you have terminated a cohabitative or "serious" relationship, some of this may apply. In any event, try to assess the dysfunctional consequences of these kinds of feelings, not only for the parties who are directly involved, but for others who are close to them.

KEY TERMS FILL-IN

1.	A _____ can be a temporary "time out" in a highly stressful marriage in order to evaluate the desirability of continuing the marriage.

2.	_____ is the legal and formal dissolution of a marriage.

3.	Monetary payments from one ex-spouse to another to maintain his or her economic needs is called _____.

4. Monetary payments by the noncustodial parent to help pay child-rearing expenses is called _____ _____.

5. In a _____-_____, guilt does not have to be established.

6. _____ _____ is the social bond that people have with others and the community.

7. According to the text, in 72 percent of the cases, the mother gets _____ of the children.

8. In _____ custody, one parent has sole responsibility for raising the child.

9. In _____ custody, the children are divided between the parents either by gender or choice.

10. In _____ custody, the children divide their time between both parents.

11. About 20 years ago _____ _____ in which a divorcing couple is assisted in coming to agreement emerged as an alternative to the usual divorce lawsuit.

MULTIPLE CHOICE

1. A trial _____ may help couples to see what living apart feels like.
   a. divorce
   b. mediation
   c. separation
   d. custody

2. The _____ separation phase is beset with problems because our society does not have clear-cut rules for this process.
   a. mid-
   b. early-
   c. pre-
   d. late-

3. During the _____ separation phase, emotional distress is compounded by the pressures of maintaining two separate households and meeting the daily emotional and physical needs of the children.
   a. mid-
   b. early-
   c. pre-
   d. late-

4. The _____ separation phase may be especially stressful for men who have been raised with traditional gender-role expectations.
   a. mid-
   b. early-
   c. pre-
   d. late-

5. According to the text, _____ is not a recent phenomenon.
   a. divorce
   b. separation
   c. alimony
   d. child support

6. Which of the following is NOT one of Bohannon's "stations of divorce"?
   a. emotional
   b. circumstantial
   c. coparental
   d. community

7. _____ is/are the monetary payment(s) for maintenance of the economic needs of one ex-spouse by the other.
   a. Property settlements
   b. Child support
   c. Palimony
   d. Alimony

8. The money payment to cover the child-rearing expenses incurred by the custodial parent is called:
   a. property settlement.
   b. child support.
   c. palimony.
   d. alimony.

9. Changes in legal, religious, and family institutions have affected _____ rates.
   a. separation
   b. marriage
   c. divorce
   d. cohabitation

10. A number of social scientists contend that _____ discourages divorce.
    a. social integration
    b. codependency
    c. sole custody
    d. alimony

11. Today, women in the United States are _____ men to seek divorce
    a. less likely than
    b. equally as likely as
    c. twice as likely as
    d. four times as likely as

12. The text points out that self-help books concerning the divorce process and television programs like "Divorce Court" have encouraged society to view divorce as:
    a. normal.
    b. an anomaly.
    c. stigmatized.
    d. undesirable.

13. Marital disruption is significantly more likely in families where children are:
    a. less than 3 years of age.
    b. between 5 and 7 years of age.
    c. 13 years of age or older.
    d. undesirable.

14. A national study of men and women 25 to 34 years of age found that the likelihood of the first marriage ending in divorce is lower for those with a bachelor's degree than for those with:
    a. only a high school degree.
    b. two years of post-graduate work.
    c. a Master's Degree
    d. a Ph.D.

15. In a national survey of adults, Patterson and Kim (1991) found that _____ is/are the number one reason for divorce.
    a. children
    b. communication problems
    c. money
    d. employment problems.

16. The text discusses the components of "divorce hangover." Which of the following is NOT one of these components?
    a. using the children
    b. throwing out everything
    c. living vicariously
    d. excessive benevolence toward others

17. Despite the institution of no-fault divorce and evidence that very few women receive substantial cash payments in a divorce, many people still believe that many women profit through divorce by high alimony payments. Weitzman dubbed this supposition the:
    a. "no-fault stigma."
    b. "equal pay for equal divorce myth."
    c. "alimony myth."
    d. "money-pit myth."

18. The _____ may feel shut out of the family and distance himself physically and/or emotionally from his children.
    a. overextended parent
    b. parent in pain
    c. revengeful parent
    d. irresponsible parent

19. According to the text, in those cases that are contested, mothers win _____ more than 70 percent of the time.
    a. alimony
    b. child support
    c. custody
    d. property settlements

20. _____ custody is when one parent has custody of the children.
    a. Sole
    b. Joint
    c. Split
    d. Divided

21. In _____ custody, sometimes called *dual residence*, the children divide their time between both parents, who share in the decisions about their upbringing.
    a. sole
    b. split
    c. joint
    d. divided

22. Opponents of _____ custody argue that it creates loyalty conflicts between the children.
    a. sole
    b. joint
    c. split
    d. divided

23. Fassel has proposed five types of divorce (*Critical Issues: "Children of Divorce"*) and subsequent effects on children. Which of the following is NOT one of these types?
    a. the disappearing parent
    b. the surprise divorce
    c. protect-the-kids divorce
    d. the see-you-later divorce

24. _____ assumes that divorcing couples can work together to benefit both parents and children.
    a. Marital counseling
    b. Divorce mediation
    c. Divorce arbitration
    d. Economic counseling

25. According to the text, the major positive outcome of divorce is that it:
    a. provides options to people in unsatisfactory marriages.
    b. eliminates unhappiness.
    c. ensures healthy parenting.
    d. limits mental illness.

ANSWERS

KEY TERMS FILL-IN

ANSWERS	PAGE NUMBERS
1. separation	396
2. Divorce	397
3. alimony	399
4. child support	399
5. no-fault	401
6. Social integration	403
7. custody	412
8. sole	413
9. split	413
10. joint	413
11. divorce mediation	422

MULTIPLE CHOICE

ANSWERS		PAGE NUMBERS
1.	c	396
2.	b	396-397
3.	a	397
4.	d	397
5.	a	397-398
6.	b	398-400
7.	d	399
8.	b	399
9.	c	400
10.	a	403
11.	c	403
12.	a	404
13.	c	404
14.	a	406
15.	b	406
16.	d	408
17.	c	409
18.	b	411
19.	c	413
20.	a	413

REMARRIAGE AND STEPFAMILIES: LIFE AFTER DIVORCE

CHAPTER OBJECTIVES

Based upon their reading and careful consideration of Chapter Sixteen students should:

1. be familiar with the rates and demographics of remarriage in American society.

2. be able to compare first marriages to remarriages.

3. understand the process of courtship after divorce.

4. be familiar with remarriage as a process, including Goetting's application of Bohannon's six stations of divorce to the remarriage process.

5. understand the relationship between remarriage and marital satisfaction.

6. understand the diversity of stepfamilies, including the different types of stepfamilies that have been identified.

7. be familiar with the ways in which stepfamilies differ from intact nuclear families and the negative image of stepfamilies.

8. be familiar with the characteristics of stepfamilies.

9. be able to identify the difficulties involved in merging two households, including the lack of institutional support, resource depletion, relationships with the children, and interpersonal relationships between the partners.

10. be familiar with the characteristics and rewards of successful remarriages and stepfamilies.

192

CHAPTER OVERVIEW

WHAT IS A STEPFAMILY? HOW COMMON IS REMARRIAGE?

A stepfamily is a household in which there is an adult couple and at least one of whom has a child from a previous marriage. Terms often used interchangeably with "stepfamily" include blended family, reconstituted family, and binuclear family. (Note: Some researchers avoid using the term "blended" because it connotes an unrealistic expectation that families can become truly blended into one, which is often not the case.) Regardless of the term used, a stepparent and stepchild do not have to live together all of the time or even part of the time to have a relationship and to share stepfamily membership.

The most dramatic changes in family structure and composition are due to remarriage and the formation of stepfamilies. The United States has the highest remarriage rate in the world; the rate is erratic, having peaked in the mid-1940s, 1950s and 1960s, but having declined steadily since about 1967. Over 40 percent of marriages are remarriages for one or both partners.

COURTSHIP AFTER DIVORCE

Ahrons (1994) wrote that "It's not unusual to see women and men frantically dating in the first year after their separation, trying to fill the void with an intense new love or even with just another warm body." Typically, the longer one has been married, the more awkward dating can be for men and women as they may feel insecure about new dating patterns. Dating may also be more awkward for older men or women. Some parents who date frequently may feel guilty about being unavailable to their children.

Custodial mothers sometimes rush into a new marriage because they want their children to have a father figure and male model. (The women may be seen as less attractive dating partners, however, by men who don't want parental responsibilities.) Although some custodial parents delay dating out of fear it will further disrupt their children's lives, some research suggests delaying dating may increase rather than decrease future problems. It appears this happens because daily family routines become more entrenched as time goes by, and changing accepted routines and rules might be especially stressful for young adolescents. It may be less disruptive for children to move into a remarriage household relatively quickly after divorce than to establish a stable single-parent household only to have that stability disrupted by another transition.

Many divorced couples have very short dating and engagement periods. Some people may rush through the courtship process because they feel they are running out of time or are desperate for financial or child-rearing help. Others may believe that they don't need as much time to get to know each other because they have learned how to avoid past mistakes. (Such assumptions are often wrong.)

REMARRIAGE: CHARACTERISTICS, PROCESS, AND SATISFACTION

Remarriage rates vary by sex, race, age, and marital status. Men remarry more quickly than do women; remarriage rates are much higher for white women than for black and Hispanic-American women; and women with low incomes and lower educational levels are the most likely to remarry. On the other hand, in general, the more money a divorced man has, the more likely he is to remarry. The majority of divorced men and women remarry other divorced people.

There are several important differences between first marriages and remarriages. First, the composition of the family may change dramatically because remarriages often result in myriad new relationships. Second, the expectations for stepfamily roles are not defined in terms of normative behavior. Third, family members may be at different stages of the life cycle and have different goals. Fourth, remarriages are structurally different from first marriages because they bring together members from at least two other families, creating a unique set of strengths and problems. Fifth, people in first marriages and remarriages may have different goals and emotional experiences. Finally, children may not want to be part of the new family.

Like divorce, remarriage is a process, but remarriage is more complicated than divorce. The remarriage process may involve as many as six stages, similar to Bohannon's six stations of divorce: emotional remarriage, psychic remarriage, community remarriage, parental remarriage, economic remarriage, and legal remarriage. Some of these phases occur independent of the existence of children, whereas others assume the involvement of children.

The data on marital satisfaction in remarriages are mixed, primarily because much of the research in this area is still fairly recent and compares stepfamilies to first marriages. Besides family structure and composition, the internal dynamics of the remarried couple are important in marital satisfaction. According to Ihinger-Tallman, the instability of a remarriage may reflect failure in one of four main areas: commitment, cohesion, communication, and the maintenance of the family's boundaries.

194

STEPFAMILIES ARE DIVERSE AND COMPLEX

Figure 16.3 provides a genogram which presents a picture of the possible family systems when two people who have been married before and have children from previous marriages marry each other (page 434).

Stepfamilies can vary in terms of parent-child relationships. The three most common types of stepfamilies are the biological mother – stepfather family, the biological father – stepmother family, and the joint biological stepfamily.

The myth of the "evil stepmother" has more recently been replaced by the "myth of instant love." This myth maintains not only that remarriage creates an instant family but that stepmothers will automatically love their stepchildren because mothering comes easily and naturally to all women. The power of the myths and unsubstantiated beliefs can be seen in the fact that adults often enter relationships with stepchildren with unrealistic expectations. Three common misconceptions about stepmothering are: 1) the stepchildren will have little effect on the new marriage; 2) we will all be one big happy family; and 3) we will both love our stepchildren as though they were our own (Burns, 1985). Many men also have unrealistic expectations about their families.

Stepfamilies may look like intact nuclear families, but they are different from these nuclear families in at least 12 ways: Stepfamilies have a complex structure; a stepfamily must fulfill different and unique tasks; stepfamilies have more stress than do nuclear families; satisfactory stepfamily integration generally takes years rather than months to achieve; very often, important relationships may be cut off or end abruptly; there may be continual transitions; there is less cohesiveness in stepfamilies than in nuclear or single-parent households; there is a great variety of patterns in stepfamily households; there are many unrealistic expectations; there is no shared family history; there are many loyalty conflicts; and roles in the stepfamily are ambiguous.

There are a number of problems in merging two households after a remarriage. Four of the most common problems are a lack of institutional support, the distribution of resources, the integration of children into the family, and the couple's interpersonal relationship.

SUCCESSFUL REMARRIAGES AND STEPFAMILIES

In a review of the literature, Visher and Visher suggest that six characteristics are common to remarried families in which children and adults experience warm interpersonal relationships and satisfaction with their lives. First, successful stepfamilies have developed realistic expectations; second, adults in these families have allowed the children involved to mourn their losses; third, the adults in these families forge a strong couple relationship; fourth, the stepparenting role proceeds slowly; fifth, successful stepfamilies develop their own rituals; and finally, these families work out satisfactory arrangements between the children's households.

Couples typically describe their remarriage as offering many more benefits than their first marriage. Reactions from stepparents are more mixed. Despite the ups and downs, a stepfamily provides members with opportunities that may be missing in an unhappy, intact family. One of the greatest benefits of remarriage and stepparenting is the opportunity to become more flexible and to learn patience.

CURRENT APPLICATIONS

1. We live in a society where close to one-half of all marriages eventually end in divorce, but in the same society, nearly half of all marriages are remarriages. This surely seems ironic, since one might suggest that those men and women who divorce would be "soured" on marriage and decide to remain single. Why is marriage so popular in American society? Make a list of those factors that serve to motivate divorced men and women to remarry.

2. Social scientists and other observers have commented that family life for remarried couples often differs sharply from that of first marriages. These commentators suggest that the primary reason for this involves the absence of socially prescribed and clearly understood guidelines for relationships within remarriages. As the text points out, remarriages are usually more complex than first marriages, especially if children are present. Proceeding from the text's discussion of the differences between first marriages and remarriages, try to construct some social guidelines for remarried relationships. To do this, first think in terms of how remarried people feel in view of current social norms. Then, give some thought to how these norms might be altered or modified.

3. Over the past two decades, there has been a lot of controversy within the social sciences about what description is most appropriate for "stepfamilies." In fact, some observers have opted for simply referring to these family units with the traditional "stepfamily" label. In tracing the history of this controversy,

however, at one time, these families were referred to as "reconstituted." Critics eventually argued that this wasn't accurate because these families really aren't "reconstituted" at all. Then, the label "blended" was proposed and used for a number of years. But, critics argued that this seemed inaccurate because very often, the families did not reflect a "blend," but rather seemed to imply *conflict*. Can you think of more appropriate, yet equally accurate characterization of these families?

4.   Stepfamilies have a number of unique characteristics there is a biological parent outside of the stepfamily unit and an adult of the same sex as the absent parent in the household; most stepchildren relate to two different households with separate rule systems; stepparents have inadequate role models; remarried families typically have diverse historical backgrounds; the children in stepfamilies have at least one extra set of grandparents—based on the work of Emily Visher and John Visher, *Stepfamilies: A Guide to Working with Stepparents and Stepchildren*, New York: Brunner/Mazel, 1979). In the previous application, you were asked to consider how social norms might be changed to "make life easier" for the members of remarried families. Now consider how the characteristics of stepfamilies conflict with existing social norms.

KEY TERMS FILL-IN

1.   Due to remarriage, children may suddenly find themselves with _____ _____ with whom they share one biological parent.

2.   A _____ is a household in which there is an adult couple and at least one of the partners has a child from a previous marriage.

3.   A _____ is a diagram showing the biological relationships among family members.

4.   In the _____ _____-_____ family, all the children are biological children of the mother and stepchildren of the father.

5.   In the _____ _____-_____ family, all the children are biological children of the father and the stepchildren of the mother.

197

6. In the _____ _____-stepfamily at least one child is the biological child of both parents, at least one child is a biological child of one parent and a stepchild of the other parent, and no other type of child is present.

MULTIPLE CHOICE

1. _____ percent of today's youth are stepsons or stepdaughters.
    a. About 15
    b. Close to 25
    c. Approximately 40
    d. More than 50

2. Seventy-five percent of women and 83 percent of men remarry within _____ years after a divorce.
    a. 1
    b. 3
    c. 5
    d. 6

3. In general, males _____ more quickly than do females.
    a. divorce
    b. separate
    c. remarry
    d. date

4. _____ rates are much higher for white women than for African- and Hispanic-American women in every age group.
    a. Remarriage
    b. Divorce
    c. Separation
    d. Desertion

5. Remarriage may result in a child having brothers and sisters, known as _____, with whom they share only one biological parent.
    a. quarter siblings
    b. half siblings
    c. unrelated siblings
    d. non-biological siblings

6.   According to the text's discussion of remarriage:
     a.   remarriage rates increase with age for both men and women.
     b.   women remarry more quickly and more often than men do.
     c.   whites are less likely to remarry than other racial-ethnic groups, and blacks are the most likely to remarry.
     d.   none of the above

7.   The text points out that:
     a.   the majority of divorced men and women remarry other divorced people.
     b.   widowers tend to remarry sooner than divorced men.
     c.   widows are slow to remarry.
     d.   all of the above

8.   There are few social guidelines for:
     a.   remarriage.
     b.   divorce.
     c.   separation.
     d.   post-divorce dating.

9.   The _____ remarriage is often a slow process in which a divorced person reestablishes a bond of attraction, commitment and trust with a member of the opposite sex.
     a.   community
     b.   parental
     c.   emotional
     d.   economic

10. The _____ remarriage is the process of changing the conjugal identity from that of individuals to couples.
     a.   psychic
     b.   parental
     c.   emotional
     d.   economic

11. _____ remarriage represents a transitional step whereby a person often must make changes in the community of friends.
     a.   Community
     b.   Parental
     c.   Emotional
     d.   Economic

12. The _____ remarriage is necessary if there are children.
    a. community
    b. parental
    c. emotional
    d. economic

13. The _____ remarriage is the reestablishment of a marital household as a unit of economic productivity and consumption.
    a. economic
    b. parental
    c. legal
    d. community

14. The _____ remarriage raises such questions as which wife deserves the life and accident insurance, medical coverage, retirement benefits, pension rights, and property rights.
    a. community
    b. parental
    c. legal
    d. economic

15. Which of the following is NOT one of the types of stepfamilies discussed in the text?
    a. biological mother-stepfather family
    b. biological father-stepmother family
    c. joint biological-stepfamily
    d. sociological stepfamily

16. When both adults have children from a previous marriage, researchers have referred to the family as a:
    a. joint biological stepfamily.
    b. serial marriage.
    c. biological stepfamily.
    d. complex stepfamily.

17. The text points out that the recent myth of "_____" maintains not only that remarriage creates an instant family, but that stepmothers will automatically love their stepchildren because mothering comes easily and naturally to all women.
    a. instant love
    b. biological affection
    c. mother-mandated affection
    d. evolutionary love

18. According to the text, stepmothers tend to have one of three common misconceptions about stepmothering. Which of the following is NOT one of these three misconceptions?
    a. The stepchildren will have little impact on the new marriage.
    b. We will all be one big, happy family.
    c. We will both love our stepchildren as though they were our own.
    d. The stepchildren will not love me.

19. According to the text's discussion of stepfamilies:
    a. satisfactory stepfamily integration usually takes a matter of months.
    b. stepfamilies usually possess a shared family history.
    c. these units have a complex structure.
    d. all of the above

20. In discussing the characteristics of stepfamilies, the text points out that:
    a. in stepfamilies, there are continual transitions instead of stability.
    b. it is normal and even desirable for stepfamily members to have unrealistic expectations.
    c. loyalty conflicts are rare in stepfamilies.
    d. none of the above

21. Which of the following is NOT one of the characteristics of stepfamilies identified in the text?
    a. Important relationships may be cut off or end abruptly.
    b. There may be continual transitions.
    c. Stepfamilies are usually more cohesive than nuclear or single-parent households.
    d. Stepfamilies vary greatly in terms of their patterns of everyday life.

22. The characterizations of stepfamilies in the text include all of the following EXCEPT:
    a. there is no shared family history.
    b. there are many loyalty conflicts.
    c. stepfamily roles are often ambiguous.
    d. stepfamily members rarely, if ever, have unrealistic expectations.

23. Which of the following is NOT one of the stages of the stepfamily cycle, as identified by clinician Patricia Papernow (*Changes*)?
    a.   fantasy
    b.   immersion
    c.   conflict resolution
    d.   resolution

24. Which of the following is NOT one of the suggestions offered by Emily and John Visher to remarried partners for dealing with sexual boundaries in the stepfamily (*Choices*)?
    a.   Do not relinquish any intimate behavior with children after they turn 10 to 11 years of age.
    b.   Be affectionate and tender but not passionate with each other when the children are with you.
    c.   Don't be sexually provocative.
    d.   Do not tolerate sexual involvement in your home.

25. Which of the following is NOT one of the "ten commandments of stepparenting" (*Choices*)?
    a.   Provide neutral territory.
    b.   Always employ "tough love."
    c.   Avoid mealtime misery.
    d.   Maintain the primacy of the marital relationship.

ANSWERS

KEY TERMS FILL-IN

ANSWERS		PAGE NUMBERS
1.	half siblings	429
2.	stepfamily	426
3.	genogram	434
4.	biological mother-stepfather	434
5.	biological father-stepmother	434
6.	joint biological	435

MULTIPLE CHOICE

ANSWERS		PAGE NUMBERS
1.	d	427
2.	b	426
3.	c	428
4.	a	428
5.	b	429
6.	d	428
7.	d	429
8.	a	430
9.	c	431
10.	a	431
11.	a	431
12.	b	431
13.	a	431
14.	c	433
15.	d	434
16.	d	435
17.	a	435
18.	d	436
19.	c	436-440
20.	a	436-440
21.	c	436-440
22.	d	436-440
23.	c	438
24.	a	441
25.	b	444

AGING AND FAMILY LIFE: GRANDPARENTS, THE WIDOWED, AND CAREGIVERS

17

CHAPTER OBJECTIVES

Based upon their reading and careful consideration of Chapter Seventeen, students should:

1. be familiar with U.S. population trends as they relate to the proportion of the elderly to the young—the rise of multigenerational families.

2. be able to identify and discuss the various aging tasks, including changes in health, stereotypes, and retirement.

3. be familiar with the different styles of grandparenting and the effects on grandparents of their children's divorce.

4. understand the different relationships between elderly parents and adult children and the implications of multigenerational families.

5. be able to compare and contrast the dying trajectory framework with the concept of the dying process from the point of view of the dying person and/or the survivors.

6. understand Kubler-Ross's stages of dying and be able to compare her model with Retsinas' alternative stage model for elderly people.

7. be familiar with hospice care for the dying.

8. be able to distinguish between bereavement, grief, and mourning and the components of consoling the bereaved.

9. be familiar with the rates of widowhood and widowerhood and be able to compare the coping skills of elderly widows and widowers in terms of social isolation and loneliness.

10. be able to discuss the structural variables that will affect family care giving to an elderly patient as well as various care giving styles and the joys and stresses of care giving.

CHAPTER OVERVIEW

THE RISE OF MULTIGENERATIONAL FAMILIES

Many demographers have observed that the aging of our society is occurring at a very rapid pace. One of the most dramatic signs of this process is that the proportion of people age 65 and over is increasing while the proportion of young people is decreasing. This aging phenomenon is explained by a decrease in fertility rates, an increase in life expectancy, and particularly high birth rates among certain racial-ethnic groups other than whites. By the year 2030, there will be more elderly people in the United States than young people.

AGING: CHANGES IN HEALTH AND SOCIAL STATUS

Middle-aged and older people are members of *later-life families*—those who are beyond the child rearing years and have begun to launch their children. Gerontologists emphasize that the aging population should not be lumped into one group because there is a great deal of diversity among later-life families. Although there is great diversity in the aged population, people ages 65 and over must confront such similar aging tasks as problems of physical and mental health, such as Alzheimer's disease and depression. The status of the elderly has probably declined since the turn of the century. In some cultures, the elderly still maintain a position of some influence. *Ageism* refers to discrimination against people on the basis of age, particularly those who are old. Many people age gracefully, with dignity, and maintain their sense of humor and values despite the ageism they encounter.

Retirement is a recent phenomenon; because Americans have greater life expectancy, they may well spend 20 percent of their adult life in retirement. Most African Americans retire because of poor health, and fewer African Americans are financially able to retire than whites. Retirement presents more financial problems to women than to men; retirement has an especially devastating impact on black women.

GRANDPARENTING

One of the most significant changes during the last twenty or thirty years has involved the rapid growth of the multigenerational family. Because families now frequently span three or four generations, the importance of the grandparent role has increased. There are at least five different styles of grandparenting: remote (where the grandparents and grandchildren see each other infrequently), companionate (the most common pattern), involved (where grandparents play an active role in raising their grandchildren), advisory (where the grandparent serves as an adviser), and surrogate (an emerging role where the grandparent replaces the parents in raising the grandchildren). These grandparenting styles often reflect such factors as the grandparents' age, physical proximity, and relationships with their own children, especially their daughter. Divorce creates both opportunities and dilemmas for grandparents. Many grandparent-grandchild relationships do become closer after the parents divorce and/or remarry and this closeness often continues into the grandchildren's young adulthood. On the other hand, a divorce can create unexpected financial burdens for the grandparents.

In many cases, adult children and aging parents live close enough to stay in touch on a daily basis. Reversing roles, adult daughters provide about the same amount of help to their parents whatever the parents' health, but sons tend to provide financial assistance only when parental health fails. Elderly parents generally try to avoid moving in with their children, primarily because they don't want to give up control of their own lives and lifestyles. There are certain advantages to multigenerational households, including the prospects for exchange of support and services.

DEATH AND DYING

Because of our increased life expectancy in the United States and other Western nations, death tends to occur most often among those who are quite elderly. All families must deal with the death of elderly parents. Physicians and other health-care professionals often use the term *dying trajectory* to describe the manner in which a very ill person is expected to die. An alternative to this framework is the concept of the dying process from the point of view of the dying person and/or the survivors. The best known conceptualization of the dying process has been formulated by Elizabeth Kubler-Ross, and involves the proposal of five stages of dying: denial, anger, bargaining, depression, and acceptance. Retsinas (1988) has argued that Kubler-Ross's model is not entirely applicable to the elderly. Although many elderly parents and relatives die in hospitals and nursing homes, hospice care provides an alternative by making the patient more comfortable and by providing companionship, a sense of security, and control of pain. Dealing with death involves bereavement, grief, and mourning. There are clusters or phases of grief and the intensity of a person's grief depends on the quality of the lost relationship, the age of the deceased, and the suddenness of the death.

Most people feel awkward when we attempt to console a grieving friend or relative; they want to be helpful but don't know what will help.

BEING WIDOWED

On the average, women live nearly seven years longer than men; consequently, there are more widows than widowers. Although most women outlive their husbands, both widows' and widowers' coping strategies typically involve adapting to a change in income as well as dealing with the emotional pain of losing a spouse and loneliness.

FAMILY CAREGIVING IN LATER LIFE

Children today actually provide more care to more parents over much longer periods of time than they did in the "good old days." The *sandwich generation* is composed of mid-life men and women who feel caught between meeting responsibilities to both their own children and to their aging parents. Furthermore, there is more difficulty involved with the provision of this care. As our population ages, more ailing Americans will need long-term care. Federal programs like Medicare and Medicaid do not pay for all of the services frequently required by elderly people. Care giving includes both family support systems and formal services such as day care for the elderly.

Matthews and Rosner (1988) contend that there are several care giving styles: routine (the core of the parental care system), backup, circumscribed, sporadic, and disassociation. All of these styles involve some degree of stress, but there are also joys associated with caregiving. For the most part, the primary caregivers are women: daughters, daughters-in-law, elderly sisters, and granddaughters.

CURRENT APPLICATIONS

1. As the text points out, American society is aging at an exceedingly rapid pace. Among the implications of an aging America is the liability for our social security system. Some critics have suggested that some young people who are working today may not ever receive social security benefits unless something is done to re-energize the system. If these critics are correct, you may well be among those who will work all of your life, only to receive substantially lowered benefits, or, perhaps, none at all. How does this make you feel? Does this thought motivate you to find out more about the future of social security? If so, you may wish to take it upon yourself to do just that.

2. Alzheimer's disease was first identified by the German neurologist Alois Alzheimer in 1906—almost a full century ago. In 1994, former President Ronald Reagan wrote an open letter to the nation, disclosing that he had the disease and expressing the hope that his announcement would make people more aware of this illness. Do you think that Americans are becoming more aware of Alzheimer's, or are they becoming *paranoid*? Is the media distorting the disease out of proportion? After all, people have been suffering from this disorder for a long time. To what extent has media exposure related to Alzheimer's been positive...or negative?

3. Chances are, you have had some personal experience with death during the past year or so. Depending upon how well you knew the person who died, this exercise will be more or less complete. To the extent that you are able, try to apply Kubler-Ross's stages of dying to the particular situation you are familiar with.

4. Given that people's life expectancy is increasing, you may very well be responsible for helping to take care of your parents in their old age. How do you feel that you would react to this responsibility (or, if you are involved in this situation right now, how are you reacting)? Do you perceive any stresses and strains? What kind? How do you feel you will cope with these problems?

KEY TERMS FILL-IN

1. _____ are those who study aging and the elderly.

2. Families that either are beyond the child rearing years, or are childless but beginning to plan for retirement are termed
    _____-_____ _____.

3. _____ is characterized by pervasive sadness and other negative feelings like a sense of worthlessness.

4. _____ _____ is a progressive, degenerative disorder that attacks the brain and impairs memory, thinking, and behavior.

5. _____ refers to discrimination against people on the basis of age, particularly those who are old.

6. _____ _____ is a public retirement pension system administered by the federal government.

7. Physicians and other health-care professional often use the term _____ _____ to describe the manner in which a very ill person is expected to die.

8. _____ care is implemented in a variety of settings.

9. _____ refers to the state of being deprived of a loved one by death.

10. _____ is the emotional response to bereavement.

11. _____ is the customary outward expression of grief.

12. The _____ _____ is composed of mid-life men and women who feel caught between meeting responsibilities to both their own children and to their aging parents.

MULTIPLE CHOICE

1. In 1960, nine percent of the population were age 65 and over, compared to _____ percent in 2000.
   a. 5
   b. 7
   c. 9
   d. 13

2. American children born in 1990 have an average life expectancy of _____ years.
   a. 70
   b. 73
   c. 76
   d. 79

3. It is expected that by the year 2030, both industrialized and developing countries are expected to have large percentages of people over 60 years old. This trend is referred to as:
   a. global maturation.
   b. global aging explosion.
   c. global petrification.
   d. global marginalization.

4. Those who are beyond the child rearing years and have begun to launch their children are classified as _____ families.
   a. elder-life
   b. post-children
   c. later-life
   d. middle-aged

5. _____—scientists who study aging and the elderly—emphasize that the aging population should not be lumped into one group because there is a great deal of diversity among later-life families.
   a. Gerontologists
   b. Paleontologists
   c. Archaeologists
   d. Physicians

6. _____ families are those that either are beyond the child-rearing years and have launched their children, or childless families who are beginning to plan for retirement.
   a. Modified-extended
   b. Later-life
   c. Post-nuclear
   d. Blended

7. The text points out that depression affects _____ percent of Americans age 65 or older.
   a. 5
   b. 10
   c. 15
   d. 35

8. Which of the following is NOT one of the symptoms of depression?
   a. changes in appetite and weight
   b. disturbed sleep
   c. motor retardation or agitation
   d. a desire to change life circumstances

9. _____ afflicts about 4 million U.S. elderly.
   a. Cancer
   b. Heart disease
   c. Depression
   d. Alzheimer's disease

10. Historians point out that in the past the elderly did not necessarily enjoy reverence and deferential treatment simply because of their:
    a.   education.
    b.   health.
    c.   age.
    d.   social status.

11. Which of the following is true of Alzheimer's Disease?
    a.   There is no known cure for Alzheimer's.
    b.   Even the early stages of the disease require institutionalization.
    c.   Alzheimer's is actually a form of insanity.
    d.   All of the above are true of Alzheimer's.

12. Discrimination against people on the basis of age, particularly because they are old, is called:
    a.   elderism.
    b.   ageism.
    c.   oldism.
    d.   gerontology.

13. The notion that old people are senile if they show forgetfulness, confusion, and reduced attention is called the myth of:
    a.   ageism.
    b.   old age.
    c.   Alzheimer's.
    d.   senility.

14. One of the most popular stereotypes is that older people become _____ as they age.
    a.   absent-minded
    b.   less intelligent
    c.   stubborn and ill tempered
    d.   more gentle and kind

15. Increased life expectancy means that many people now spend at least _____ percent of their adult lives in retirement.
    a.   5
    b.   10
    c.   20
    d.   40

16. Social Security benefits depend on how long people have been:
    a.   in the labor force.
    b.   educated.
    c.   retired.
    d.   unemployed.

17. Five styles of grandparenting are mentioned in the text. Which of the following is NOT one of these?
    a.   remote
    b.   hyperactive
    c.   involved
    d.   surrogate

18. According to Jendrek, there are specific categories of surrogate grandparents. Which of the following is NOT one of these?
    a.   custodial
    b.   living-with
    c.   day-care
    d.   All of the above were identified by Jendrek.

19. The text points out that the increase in grandchildren living with grandparents in "skipped generations" homes is due to:
    a.   the growth in drug use among parents.
    b.   teen pregnancy.
    c.   the death or incarceration of parents.
    d.   all of the above.

20. In the intermediate stage of _____ people often search for the dead person.
    a.   bereavement
    b.   mourning
    c.   grief
    d.   alienation

21. _____ ranges from normal grief to pathological melancholy that may include such reactions as physical or mental illness.
    a.   Bereavement
    b.   Mourning
    c.   Grief
    d.   Alienation

22. The final stage of _____ may occur from 6 months to several years after the death.
    a. recovery and reorganization
    b. alienation and apathy
    c. idealization
    d. mourning

23. Huntley (*Choices*) suggests a variety of strategies for helping children grieve. Which of the following is NOT one of these suggestions?
    a. Recognize that each child will grieve differently.
    b. Encourage the expression of feelings.
    c. Take steps to break with a normal routine.
    d. Take advantage of available resources.

24. *Thanatologists* are social scientists who study:
    a. children's grief.
    b. euthanasia.
    c. death and grief.
    d. physician-assisted suicide.

25. Which of the following is NOT one of the types of family caregiving in later life, as identified by Matthews and Rosner?
    a. affective
    b. circumscribed
    c. sporadic
    d. disassociation

ANSWERS

KEY TERMS FILL-IN

MULTIPLE CHOICE

ANSWERS   **PAGE NUMBERS**

1.	c	450
2.	c	450
3.	b	450
4.	c	451
5.	a	451
6.	b	451
7.	c	452
8.	d	452
9.	d	452
10.	c	453
11.	a	452
12.	b	454
13.	d	454
14.	c	455
15.	c	457
16.	a	457
17.	b	458-460
18.	d	461-462
19.	d	461
20.	c	466
21.	b	466
22.	a	466-467
23.	c	467
24.	c	467
25.	a	472-473

18

THE FAMILY IN THE TWENTY-FIRST CENTURY

CHAPTER OBJECTIVES

Based upon their reading and careful consideration of Chapter Eighteen, students should:

1. be familiar with the changes faced by the family of the twenty-first century, including alternations in racial-ethnic diversity, family structure, children's rights, health-related issues, economic concerns, and global aging.

2. understand the advantages and disadvantages of a national health-care policy, particularly in light of the AIDS epidemic.

3. be able to identify the economic concerns of the family in the twenty-first century in terms of poverty and gender inequality in the workplace.

4. be prepared to compare and contrast child-care and parental-leave policies in the United States with other industrialized countries.

5. understand the conditions and implications for the poor of the 1996 "Welfare Reform Act."

6. be able to identify emerging issues related to global aging as young and old compete for scarce resources.

CHAPTER OVERVIEW

In considering the family of the twenty-first century, many observers assume that the dynamic processes that have shaped the family during the past two decades will continue to do so in the future. This chapter focuses on six areas: family structure, racial-ethnic diversity, children's rights, health-related issues, economic concerns, and global aging.

FAMILY STRUCTURE

While it's likely that in the future, variations in family structures will increase in number and forms, there's no evidence that marriage will be replaced. (Although many people are cohabitating and remaining single longer, about 93 percent of Americans will marry at least once.) The family is still the primary group that provides the nurturance, love, and emotional sustenance that people use to be happy, healthy, and productive.

RACIAL-ETHNIC DIVERSITY

Racial-ethnic diversity will increase because of heavy immigration from abroad, as will higher fertility rates among African Americans and some Asian American and Latino families. (People of color currently account for 24 percent of the U.S. population and are expected to increase to 30 percent by 2020.) As minorities make up a larger share of the population and labor force, they will increase their impact on political, educational, and economic institutions. Racial-ethnic communities will continue to grow and change in the twenty-first century as well.

CHILDREN'S RIGHTS

Substantial research indicates that not only has the United States abandoned many of its children, but that the situation has been deteriorating since 1980. In 1999, almost 12 percent of children living below the poverty level experienced "moderate" or "severe" hunger.

FAMILY POLICY

Measures taken by governmental bodies to achieve specific objectives relating to the family's well being (family policy) have improved many children's lives. One bright spot cited in the text is the 1975 Child Support Enforcement Act along with amendments in 1984 that require the states to withhold monies equal to child-support obligations from wages and other income of delinquent noncustodial parents. In 1988, the Family Support Act strengthened these guidelines, requiring that judges provide a written justification for review by a higher court if they wish to depart from state guidelines in any way. Then there is the 1994 legislation that requires that states withhold funds for child-support payments in every case--not just those that are delinquent. Courts are also becoming more "child friendly" through their recognition of children's rights. Still, childcare and parental leave remain problems for American families today.

HEALTH-RELATED ISSUES

HIV and AIDS have had little effect on sexual behavior among heterosexuals. Adolescent males and females are unlikely to protect themselves; not even college students or others educated about the risks of AIDS are using condoms, even during casual sex. HIV and AIDS will also affect multigenerational families. As the AIDS virus spreads, increasing numbers of children are being orphaned and will probably be cared for by grandparents or even great-grandparents.

A second health-related issue discussed is the lack of a national health care program in the U.S. today. Despite the existence of programs like Medicaid and Medicare, almost 33 percent of the poor had no health insurance of any kind during 1999. During the same year, over 40 percent of Latinos and Asian Americans had no health insurance. The pros and cons of the Canadian health care system are discussed in this section along with the ambivalence of many Americans about a national health-care coverage program.

ECONOMIC CONCERNS

The text points out that much research suggests that poverty, especially child poverty, is not a compelling social issue in the U.S. today. One reason that has been suggested why the U.S. has the high poverty rate that it does is its failure to develop a comprehensive antipoverty agenda. It appears that child and family poverty could be alleviated if parents had jobs that paid enough.

Most Americans are recipients of welfare, either directly or indirectly. In addition to government and to those who can't support themselves because they are poor or unemployed, there are programs that help both the middle class and the wealthy that aren't called welfare. For example, the middle class can take advantage of student loans or loans to veterans. Corporate welfare (e.g. subsidizing industries) is even greater. In 1997, corporate welfare programs cost taxpayers $10 billion.

In 1996 President Clinton signed The Personal Responsibility and Work Opportunity Reconciliation Act (a.k.a. "The Welfare Reform Act") that turned control of federally financed welfare programs over to the states. The law converts AFDC (Aid to Families with Dependent Children) to a block grant called Temporary Assistance to Needy Families (TANF) and has a five-year lifetime limit on benefits for welfare recipients. The law requires welfare recipients to work after receiving two years of benefits, to enroll in on-the-job or vocational training, or to do community service. Proponents of this law have argued that the best way to get people off welfare is to require them to work. Opponents of the Welfare Reform Act of 1996 maintain that the law will increase child poverty and punishes children for their parents' economic mistakes. It is pointed out that if aid to current welfare recipients is discontinued without increasing jobs that provide a living, poverty levels will in all likelihood increase.

An ongoing problem that contributes to women's and children's economic vulnerability is the wage gap between women and men. Employment discrimination is clearly one of the factors that has helped create the sex gap in pay. One remedy to this problem may be comparable worth. Proponents argue that jobs can be measured in terms of such variables as required education, skills, experience, mental demands, and working conditions, and the inherent worth of a job. Pay adjustments based on the concept of comparable worth have only affected public-sector workers to date, because no U.S. law requires comparable worth in wages.

GLOBAL AGING

By 2000, about 7 percent of the world's population will be 65 years old or older. Such "world graying" is likely to affect both the young and old. One emerging issue in the U.S. that is related to population aging is the right-to-die movement. A discussion of this movement in the U.S. includes the viewpoints of proponents and opponents of the movement, Dr. Jack Kevorkian's physician assisted suicides, and the emergence of living wills.

Another issue discussed is the competition for scarce resources that lies ahead as the increasing numbers of older Americans will put a significant strain on the nation's health care services and retirement-income programs. Because, in general, people reaching age 65 now and in the future will be better educated and have more work-related skills than earlier cohorts, they are more likely to be productive employees. They may also offer an employer more skills than younger persons entering the workplace.

Another recommendation is lifting the penalties on older people who want to continue to work. If old age and mandatory retirement were pushed up to age 70 or higher, many productive older Americans could continue to work and contribute to Social Security.

CURRENT APPLICATIONS

1.   The text outlines a variety of changes that will affect families

during the twenty-first century. Do you find any of these alterations disturbing? How do you think you will be affected by the changes? Use your parents as a point of comparison. How do you think your family experiences will be different from theirs? In your mind, are these differences positive, negative, or indifferent?

2. Numerous critics are alarmed by the declining role of the family in American society. For example, it has been observed that couples are having fewer children because children require that parents, especially mothers, make psychic and material sacrifices in a career-oriented society. Assuming that our society maintains its extreme emphasis on careers, money, success, etc., the birth rate may continue to decline. Do you feel that there is cause for alarm? Do you think that our government may, eventually, be forced to provide *incentives* for men and women to increase the birth rate? What would be the implications of such a necessity for our society, as we know it today?

3. AIDS is obviously of great interest to you as a college student, since many college-aged men and women are not married and are sexually active. But to what extent have you really thought critically about the implications of AIDS for our society in the future? What will happen if AIDS begins to spread more and more through heterosexual contact? What will this mean for marriage and family? What kind of normative structures will likely emerge over the next 50 years in reaction to the spread of AIDS among heterosexuals?

4. The text discusses the economic concerns of the family in the twenty-first century in terms of poverty and the welfare program as it currently exists under the 1996 Welfare Reform Act. What are your feelings about the resultant changes? Also, what are your feelings about "corporate welfare"?

5. The wage gap between women and men stems from, among other things, employment discrimination. Comparable worth could have a significant effect on addressing this gender-based inequity. Discuss the question: Is *comparable worth* a realistic goal by the first part of the next century? Why or why not? Some critics have commented that the recent trend in American society toward increased conservatism and more emphasis on "traditional family values" may signal a return to traditional gender role orientation. What's your reaction to this prediction?

KEY TERMS FILL-IN

1. _____ _____ is the measure taken by governmental bodies to achieve specific objectives concerning the family's well being.

2. _____ is government aid to those who can't support themselves, generally because they are poor.

3. In 1996, President Clinton signed The Personal Responsibility and Work Opportunity Reconciliation Act that turned control of federally financed welfare programs over to the states. This act is more commonly referred to as the _____ _____ _____.

4. The federal government directly subsidizing industries or savings and loan banks when they declare bankruptcy because of fraud or widespread embezzlement is an example of _____ welfare.

5. The aging of the world population is referred to in the text as "_____ _____."

6. _____ _____ is a concept that calls for equal pay for both males and females doing work that requires similar skill, effort, and responsibility and is performed under similar working conditions.

7. A _____ _____ is a document that specifies the conditions under which people want life-support systems removed rather than to be kept alive by machines.

MULTIPLE CHOICE

1. Family policy is the measures taken by government bodies to achieve specific objectives concerning.
    a. the family's well being.
    b. child care.
    c. family size.
    d. contraception.

2. People of color currently account for _____ percent of the U.S. population.
    a. 12
    b. 24
    c. 36
    d. 48

3. According to the text, we will probably see more households that are _____ and are comprised of unrelated adults and stepfamilies.
    a. nuclear
    b. extended
    c. multigenerational
    d. homosexual

4. Many people are cohabiting and remaining single longer; however, about _____ percent marry at least once.
    a. 25
    b. 50
    c. 75
    d. 93

5. The measures taken by governmental bodies to achieve specific objectives relating to the family's well-being are known collectively as *family*:
    a. law.
    b. norms.
    c. principles.
    d. policy.

6. The Family Support Act of 1988 allowed _____ to depart from state child support guidelines only if they provide written justification that can be reviewed by a higher court.
    a. parents
    b. judges
    c. attorneys
    d. the Friend of the Court

7. In 1994, voters in the state of _____ supported a referendum to legalize assisted suicide.
    a. Ohio
    b. California
    c. Oregon
    d. Michigan

8.   In 1992, one of the best-selling books was *Final Exit,* which describes how the elderly and terminally ill can:
     a.   make a living will.
     b.   plan for retirement.
     c.   commit suicide.
     d.   avoid probate.

9.   Such organizations as Choice in Dying, the Hemlock Society, and Concern for Dying have reported widespread interest in information on:
     a.   retirement income.
     b.   living wills.
     c.   suicide.
     d.   establishing trusts.

10. Under the Welfare Reform Act of 1996, what is the lifetime limit placed on benefits for welfare recipients?
     a.   one year
     b.   two years
     c.   three years
     d.   five years

11. In Japan, _____ percent of childcare is provided by the government.
     a.   25
     b.   50
     c.   60
     d.   over 90

12. By the year 2000, almost _____ percent of Americans was 65 years of age or older.
     a.   7
     b.   12
     c.   19
     d.   26

13. According to the text, the family in the twenty-first century will:
     a.   be increasingly homogeneous.
     b.   involve considerably diversity.
     c.   have fewer choices.
     d.   incorporate fewer work roles.

14. _____ is a concept that calls for equal pay for both males and females doing work that requires equivalent skill, effort, and responsibility and is performed under similar working conditions.
    a. The deregulation of gender restrictions
    b. Comparable worth
    c. The glass ceiling
    d. The pink-collar ghetto

15. According to the text, battles over who should care for children are likely to escalate because of:
    a. archaic parental leave policies in the U.S.
    b. the lack of good childcare facilities.
    c. increased numbers of women entering the labor force or higher education.
    d. All of the above.

16. Although often applauded as a model that the U.S. should adopt, the Canadian healthcare system has been criticized for several reasons. Which of the following is NOT one of them?
    a. There is too much paperwork.
    b. High-tech resources are often scarce.
    c. The system is most effective when problems are relatively minor and people can wait for services - it does less well in emergencies.
    d. All are criticisms of the Canadian healthcare system.

17. The text suggests that most Americans have attitudes toward national health-care coverage that are:
    a. totally supportive.
    b. ambivalent due to economic uncertainty.
    c. totally opposed to it.
    d. confused due to their inability to understand how the healthcare industry operates.

18. Today, a householder would need to earn _____/hour and work full-time, 52 weeks a year to have an annual gross salary above the $17,029 income level defined as the poverty level for a family of four.
    a. $5.15
    b. $7.25
    c. $8.50
    d. $11.25

223

19. Under the 1996 "Welfare Reform Act," Temporary Assistance to Needy Families (TANF) has a _____ year lifetime limit on benefits to welfare recipients.
    a. 2
    b. 5
    c. 7
    d. 9

20. Which of the following is true about the 1996 "Welfare Reform Act"?
    a. Control of federally financed welfare remains in the hands of the federal government.
    b. The only way cash assistance can exceed current limits is if a family moves from state to state or goes off welfare and returns later.
    c. Unmarried mothers 18 years old are required to live with an adult and to attend school as a condition of receiving welfare.
    d. All of the above are true.

ANSWERS

KEY TERMS FILL-IN

ANSWERS	PAGE NUMBERS
1. Family Policy	478
2. Welfare	484
3. Welfare Reform Act	484
4. corporate	484
5. "world graying"	485
6. Comparable worth	485
7. living will	487

MULTIPLE CHOICE

ANSWERS	PAGE NUMBERS
1. a	478
2. b	477
3. c	477
4. d	477